READING THROUGH
LUKE

WITH
THE DEVOTED COLLECTIVE

The Devoted Collective
Auckland, New Zealand
www.thedevotedcollective.org

© Copyright 2023 The Devoted Collective Ltd. All rights reserved.

ISBN Hardcover 978-1-7386079-2-1

No portion of this book may be reproduced, stored in a retrieval system or transmitted in any form or by any means—electronic, mechanical, photocopy, recording or otherwise—except for brief quotations in printed reviews of promotion, without prior written permission from the author. All text in bold or in parentheses are the author's own.

Unless otherwise noted, all Scripture is taken from the New International Version®, NIV®. Copyright © 1973, 1978, 1984, 2011 by Biblica, Inc.™ Used by permission of Zondervan. All rights reserved worldwide.

Scripture quotations marked ESV are taken from the ESV® Bible (The Holy Bible, English Standard Version®). Copyright © 2001 Crossway, a publishing ministry of Good News Publishers. Used by permission. All rights reserved.

Scripture quotations marked MSG are taken from *The Message*, copyright © 1993, 2002, 2018 by Eugene H. Peterson. Used by permission of NavPress. All rights reserved. Represented by Tyndale House Publishers.

Scripture quotations taken from the (NASB®) New American Standard Bible®, Copyright © 1960, 1971, 1977, 1995, 2020 by The Lockman Foundation. Used by permission. All rights reserved. www.lockman.org

Scripture quotations marked NKJV are taken from the New King James Version. Copyright © 1982 by Thomas Nelson, Inc. Used by permission. All rights reserved.

Scripture quotations marked (NLT) are taken from the *Holy Bible*, New Living Translation, copyright ©1996, 2004, 2015 by Tyndale House Foundation. Used by permission of Tyndale House Publishers, Carol Stream, Illinois 60188. All rights reserved.

Scripture quotations marked NRSV are taken from the New Revised Standard Version Bible, copyright © 1989 National Council of the Churches of Christ in the United States of America. Used by permission. All rights reserved worldwide.

Typesetting by Holly Robertson of Design by Rocket www.designbyrocket.com
Illustrations by Audrey Powell, @audreypowell_design on Instagram
Edited by Vicki Bentley and Aimée Walker

Cataloguing in Publishing Data Title: Reading Through Luke
Author: The Devoted Collective
Subjects: Devotions, Christian life, Spirituality

A copy of this title is held at the National Library of New Zealand.

*Because of God's tender mercy,
the morning light from heaven is about to break upon us,
to give light to those who sit in darkness and in the shadow of death,
and to guide us to the path of peace.*

Luke 1:78-79 (NLT)

The Gospel of Luke opens with the heralding of the good news that is Jesus: He is "the rising sun" that has come from Heaven to illuminate the darkness engulfing the earth and to guide us back to the path God intended for us—the path of peace.

However the path of peace does not look like we expect it to, for Jesus did not come to overthrow political regimes or to take an earthly throne for Himself, but rather to proclaim and demonstrate the nearness of the Father's Kingdom. He came to seek out the lost and to lift up the humble; to draw near to the outcast, to call sinners to repentance, and to fill the hungry. He came to exemplify a life of complete surrender and obedience to the Father, while walking in step with Holy Spirit—and now He calls us to follow suit.

And so, we invite you to journey through the book of Luke with us, tracing the steps of Jesus as He journeys towards the cross in order to grasp how His life must shape our own. Each day you'll read a portion of Scripture paired with a devotion designed to help you sink deep into the Word and reflect on the ministry of Christ and the nature of His Kingdom.

It is our prayer that these words enrich your understanding of *His Word* and stir a passion in you to wholeheartedly follow after Jesus, committing your life to seeking first His Kingdom and His glory.

The Devoted Team

Contents

Day One	This is a Harvest Season Heather Carlisle	10
Day Two	Make Him Large Aimée Walker	13
Day Three	Room for All Jenna Marie Masters	16
Day Four	Always Near Adéle Deysel	19
Day Five	Good Fruit Marissa Price	22
Day Six	This is My Son Aimée Walker	25
Day Seven	New Level, New Devil Amber Palmer	28
Day Eight	I Know Who You Are Tiffany Seldon	31
Day Nine	Abandoning Self-Sufficiency Shelley Johnson	34
Day Ten	It's in the Stretch Jenna Marie Masters	37
Day Eleven	The Unshakeable Kingdom Mazhar Kefali	40
Day Twelve	Jesus Draws Near Heather Carlisle	43

Day Thirteen	Fragrant Grace Tabitha Meglich	46
Day Fourteen	Into the Light Adéle Deysel	49
Day Fifteen	Encountered Kay Gleaves	52
Day Sixteen	True Confession Tabitha Meglich	55
Day Seventeen	Kingdom Impact Kay Gleaves	58
Day Eighteen	Executive Assistants Emily Tyler	61
Day Nineteen	Choose the Better Shelley Johnson	64
Day Twenty	Teach us to Pray Tiffany Seldon	67
Day Twenty-One	God-Blessed Eyes Emily Tyler	70
Day Twenty-Two	No Reason to Fear Paula Morrison	73
Day Twenty-Three	Dressed and Ready Vicki Bentley	76
Day Twenty-Four	True Friends Rebekah Bermingham	79
Day Twenty-Five	Table Talk Tabitha Meglich	82

Day Twenty-Six	Lost and Found Paula Morrison	85
Day Twenty-Seven	Wise Wealth Victoria Stewart Malone	88
Day Twenty-Eight	Unlimited Forgiveness Dan Tyler	91
Day Twenty-Nine	Upside Down Shelley Johnson	94
Day Thirty	Again and Again and Again Emily Tyler	97
Day Thirty-One	Fulfilled Marissa Price	100
Day Thirty-Two	Proverbial Fences Dan Tyler	103
Day Thirty-Three	The Attention of the King Heather Carlisle	106
Day Thirty-Four	Our Sanctuary Aimée Walker	109
Day Thirty-Five	Sifted Like Wheat Mazhar Kefali	112
Day Thirty-Six	The Cup of Life Amber Palmer	115
Day Thirty-Seven	The Paradoxical King Victoria Stewart Malone	118
Day Thirty-Eight	Outrageous Love Vicki Bentley	121

Day Thirty-Nine	Polishing the Prophecies Mazhar Kefali	124
Day Forty	Move Forward in Peace Emily Tyler	127

DAY ONE
This is a Harvest Season
HEATHER CARLISLE

Luke 1:1-45

Has an area of your life ever seemed so unfruitful that it made you feel ashamed? Like anytime the topic comes up in conversation, you want to run and hide? I know I have. Barrenness and disgrace were two themes that were woven together in Jesus' time, too. The cultural belief then was that a barren woman must not have the Lord's blessing; she must have some hidden sin causing this condition. And while this isn't the case with physical barrenness so much anymore, thank God, I do think some scepticism still exists in relation to other areas of barrenness in our lives. We feel the pressure from ourselves and others: *Why after all these years of prayer is my husband unchanged? Why can't I figure out what's wrong in my body and get healthy? After all I've sown selflessly for years into this friendship, why am I never seeing the love returned? What am I doing wrong?!*

In this first chapter of Luke we meet Zechariah the priest and his wife Elizabeth who were advanced in years and unable to have children. What a disgraceful weight to carry as a priest in that culture! Surely many thought, *If he wasn't properly atoning for his own family's sin, could he really be trusted with atoning for others?* I love that God sets the record straight for us in verse 6: "Both of them were righteous in the sight of God, observing all the Lord's commands and decrees blamelessly." Righteous and blameless, their lack of harvest had nothing to do with their sins and flaws, and God decided to move on their behalf to prove it.

Sometimes we internalise blame without even realising it. After experiencing a very tough newborn stage with my second baby who was born with reflux and severe allergies, I had unconsciously begun to carry the weight of guilt. It took opening a conversation with the Lord about that traumatic season for Him to whisper to my heart, "This wasn't your fault." Maybe you need to hear that from Heaven over circumstances in your life too: You are righteous and blameless.

Not every mess is your fault!

In verse 25, we see how God removes their shame by giving Zechariah and Elizabeth the gift of a son—John the Baptist who would pave the way for the Son of God. God loves to save the very best gifts for those who have waited long and endured much suffering and shame. He is the same God today. One moment of favour with God is often all that is needed to change the narrative.

We see this same theme as we read the parallel story of Elizabeth's cousin, Mary. She is given the honour of carrying the Son of God in her womb, and she too is "highly favoured" (v.28). Through Jesus, we all have God's favour resting upon us. We can open up our hearts to hear from Heaven the same words the Father said over Jesus: "This is my beloved child in whom I'm well pleased" (Luke 3:22 ESV).

As I consider the theme of barrenness and disgrace in this chapter, I feel the Spirit stirring me that this is a harvest season. In places where you have felt an ache of emptiness, God wants to fill you to overflowing. In places where you have sown in tears, you will reap in joy. You will see the prophet Isaiah's words that "The Lord will surely comfort Zion and will look with compassion on all her ruins; he will make her deserts like Eden, her wastelands like the garden of the Lord. Joy and gladness will be found in her, thanksgiving and the sound of singing" (Isaiah 51:3). Just like with the blessing of John the Baptist to his parents, this abundance may look different than you thought or may even involve some earthly suffering. But rest assured, the harvest He is pouring out will be great in the eyes of the Lord! It will bring Him glory! And what favour the Father shows us in inviting us to play a part!

Where in your life are you still waiting to see a harvest? Have you inadvertently started to believe that the delay is your fault? Spend some time in stillness before the Father. What truth is He whispering to your heart? Thank Him in advance for the blessings that are still to come.

DAY TWO

AIMÉE WALKER

Luke 1:46-80

I have a tendency to break out into song lyrics that drives my kids crazy. When I'm over-tired, I sing, when I'm happy, I sing, and when I'm trying to diffuse an argument, I've been known to break out into the chorus of the Spice Girls hit-song, "Stop." And as much as it annoys them, it also works. The fights end and are replaced by eye-rolls and groans about how ridiculous their mother is. There's something about the marriage of music and lyric that has the power to shift an atmosphere, releasing joy, hope, and peace. It's no wonder that the pages of Scripture are filled with well over one hundred and eighty-five songs—four of which are found in Luke's Gospel, and all in the first two chapters!

However, it's not so much the song itself that holds the power, as it is its subject. And that's why "Mary's Song," often referred to as the "Magnificat" has endured through the ages. It gained this name because the verb, *megalynō*, which she uses in verse 46 where she proclaims, "my soul glorifies the Lord," literally means 'to magnify, to show great,' or my favourite, 'to make large'. I still remember the first time I heard Mary's declaration of praise incorporated into Hillsong's popular worship song, "Exceeding Joy" and how it caused my own heart to glory in the truth that a holy mighty God was mindful of me. I, too, desired to 'make Him large'.

As she reflects on the wonder that God has chosen her, a young unknown girl from an off-the-grid town to carry the Messiah, and the reality that "from now on all generations will call [her] blessed" (v.48), Mary finds herself recalling God's faithfulness throughout the ages and the way He has helped her people, Israel. She is mindful of both His mercy (vv.50 and 54) and His power (v.51), and her words demonstrate not only a deep understanding of Scripture, but also of God's nature and His ways. She understands that this is a God whose ways are not our own (Isaiah 55:8-9): He opposes the proud and lifts up the humble (vv.51-52); He fills the hungry and sends the rich away empty-handed, always remembering His covenant to Abraham and His descendants (vv.54-55).

Similarly, Zechariah's song also invites us to remember the faithful, covenant-keeping nature of our God (vv.72-73). As a new covenant is on the threshold of being ushered in, he, too, 'makes large' God, celebrating all that the Lord has done for his family and for Israel. But on closer reading, we see that Zechariah's song is both praise and prophecy. Zechariah is not simply reflecting on what God has done for Israel, He is also looking forward to what He *will* do as He raises up the "horn of salvation," Jesus (v.69). But so confident is he in what the future holds, that he speaks in the past tense as though it were already fully accomplished: "He *has* come" and "He *has* redeemed" and "He *has* raised up a horn of salvation" (vv.68-69).

Zechariah was confident God could be trusted to do what He had promised, because like Mary, he understood that God doesn't always work in the way that we expect Him to or think He should. While Israel anticipated a political saviour who would overthrow the Roman oppressors, Zechariah knew who the true enemy was: sin. And that the redemption they ultimately needed was the forgiveness of their sins so that they could serve the Lord "without fear in holiness and righteousness" (vv.74-75). So he prophesies over his newborn son, declaring that he will be the one to go before and prepare the way for the people to receive their promised salvation (vv.76-77), that the light might shine in the darkness (v.79).

There are many parallels between Mary and Zechariah's songs, but perhaps one of the most striking is how rich they both are in Scripture and theology—line after line drips with Old Testament references and covenantal promises. The Word and their history with God fuelled their worship and the same must be true for us. As we steep ourselves in the truth of God's Word and rehearse our testimonies and the testimonies of those who have gone before us, the fruit should be worship. The fruit should be lives and 'songs' that make Him large and thereby allow others to glimpse the light that has graciously enabled us to walk "the path of peace" (v.79).

Take some time to intentionally make God large in your heart today. Write a list of the things He has done for you and the verses that inspire you to worship and give Him the praise that He is due.

DAY THREE
Room For All
JENNA MARIE MASTERS

Luke 2:1-20

The rowdy audience suddenly hushed. It was a stuffy ninety-eight degrees, and the stench of egg salad elbowed its way down the aisle. I felt a bit nauseated, but every annoyance faded when a ten-year-old girl catapulted off her seat and shouted, "I have to get baptised! Like, right now!" Our eyes locked, and I couldn't help but tear up. She had given her heart to Jesus weeks before and meant business.

You may imagine this scene took place during Sunday school, but instead it played out on the side of the road in an old trailer outside a public school. It was my first year teaching Chapel on Wheels—a program available in some American schools where, with their parents' permission, kids trek out to a hot, crowded trailer to hear about Jesus. Here, church and state are separated by twelve inches out on the curb. All across the nation, kids give up their lunch recess to participate. *Why?*

To know they're loved by their Creator. To believe they matter.

One week, a woman peeked in and questioned, "Is this a church?!" "Well, kind of," I answered. "For forty-five minutes, it's church to these kids." She threw her hands up, "Can you believe it? They took God out of the schools and kicked Him out on the street!" It made me laugh out loud. It *does* sound sad, but God can't be kicked out of any place. Satan is a liar.

Joseph was told there was no room at the inn for Jesus to be born (Luke 2:6-7). But no room did *not* mean no Jesus. The angel declared to the shepherds, "I am bringing you good news of great joy for all the people" (v.11 ESV). The nature of Jesus' birth proclaimed that even if you have no room for Him, He has made room for you—for *all* people: the lowly, the broken, the humble, the shamed. He came to redeem and restore *everyone*.

We may not like the thought of our precious King being born in an animal stable. He deserved to enter this world in the most lavish circumstances, surrounded by honour. But Jesus didn't come to get what He deserved; He came for those who felt deserted. If He was born the way a King ought to be, shepherds wouldn't have run in darkness to see God's face, and fishermen would never have called Him, "friend."

It wasn't that Jesus was born outside of a worthy kingdom, rather His manner of birth and life defined what a worthy kingdom looks like. He came outside the world's expectations so everyone who wanted to find Him could. But our merciful Saviour also came for those who didn't want to find Him. And He would willingly wait a foot away from their heart-wrenching defiance—even if told there is no room for Him.

Just as they remained in Bethlehem, waiting for Jesus to arrive, we can follow Joseph and Mary's example to be obedient to where God calls us. Sometimes, God will call us to remain near walls, circumstances, and friendships that have no room for Jesus. I encourage you to stand firm and not give up on them! God knows you love them; He loves them more and wants to be delivered into their hearts. He may be asking you to be the midwife. Jesus is coming!

A stinky stable didn't keep kings, wise men, and shepherds from coming to see Jesus. And apparently, a stinky trailer won't keep rowdy fifth graders from Him, either! God can do His thing anywhere. "KEEP OUT" signs are really "KEEP PRAYING" signs. We can sit outside public schools, government buildings, broken relationships—and pray. No wall, law, or enemy can keep Jesus out, especially when we are obedient in doing what He asks of us!

Twenty kids accepted Jesus as Lord in our funky little trailer that year. We didn't have to go into the school that kept Jesus out; we simply had to nestle ourselves against the cold curb and deliver Jesus to them. He came.

Despite rejection or 'keep out' signs, where are you divinely positioned to stay and pray? Ask Holy Spirit to show you those that are in desperate need of receiving God's love and make it a priority to bring them before the Lord today.

DAY FOUR

Always Near
ADÉLE DEYSEL

Luke 2:21-52

While my mom and I were distracted in the clothing aisles of Kmart, I was under the impression that my husband and mom-in-law were keeping an eye on my four-year-old daughter. A casual check-in with my husband, however, confirmed this was not the case, and we had all inadvertently taken our eyes off her. As a parent, nothing prepares you for the fear that grips your heart and the panic that overwhelms you like a flash flood when you are faced with the stark reality that your child is gone! Dark thoughts seized my mind as we called out her name and ran in different directions frantically searching for her. When we finally found her, with my heart still pounding and tears of relief flowing, I held my little girl so tightly she complained. She was blissfully unaware of the momentary chaos that had unfolded around her.

Our ordeal may have been over in minutes, but Mary and Joseph searched for three days before they found Jesus. On their journey back to Nazareth after the Passover festival in Jerusalem (Luke 2:41-52), they incorrectly assume that their twelve-year-old son is somewhere among the crowd of people that are travelling with them. Absorbed in the companionship of family and friends, they settle into the familiarity of their annual 192km walk, perhaps busying themselves with the 'to-do lists' of setting up camp. One day into their journey, however, they realise they have lost Jesus and an anxious search ensues (v.48). Panic and fear must have gripped their hearts for the three days they were looking for their son.

But Jesus did not have the same experience. He did not consider Himself 'lost' and was surprised that they didn't know where to find Him. Jesus was exactly where He was supposed to be—in "His Father's house" (v.49).

Mary and Joseph's anxious search originated because they took their eyes off Jesus. With their focus divided, they became less vigilant and inevitably lost sight of their son. The same can also be true of us. We can find ourselves busy and distracted by the checklists of life as we attempt to keep our pain and fear at bay. We frantically search for meaning and purpose and even in our endeavours to serve the Lord, we can assume that Jesus is still walking with us, instead of choosing to intentionally walk *with Him*.

The moment we recognise feelings of anxiety, panic, and fear, we need to stop and ask ourselves when we last connected with Jesus. Not just a routine devotion or prayer but a true connection that leaves us refreshed and transformed. And when we start retracing our steps back to Jesus with a humble posture of worship and surrender...

We find He is exactly where we last met Him.

Jesus does not leave us; we walk away from Him. But no matter how far we wander, He is always near. Through His death and resurrection, Jesus made a way for us to approach the Father with freedom and confidence (Ephesians 3:12). It is in our restored intimate personal relationship with God the Father, Son, and Holy Spirit that we find love (John 3:16), joy (John 20:20), and the purpose we crave (Ephesians 1:3-5).

No worldly pursuit will satisfy our needs. But relentlessly chasing a transformative relationship with Jesus will limit distraction, confusion, and overfamiliarity and realign our lives with the hope and future that God has planned for us (Jeremiah 29:11). Regardless of our circumstances, with our eyes fixed on Him we will know with certainty He is always with us on the journey.

What currently has your attention and focus? Is it drawing you closer to the Lord, or causing you to wander? Allow Holy Spirit to show you what distractions need to be eliminated to enable you to keep in step with Jesus so you can live into all He has prepared for you.

DAY FIVE
Good Fruit
MARISSA PRICE

Luke 3:1-20

There is a grand sense of pause between chapters two and three of Luke that almost feels as though an intermission has taken place. The first few verses help to set the scene by indicating who is ruling at this point in history. John is then introduced to us as a messenger who has heard the word of God in the wilderness and is responding to that word by proclaiming the good news of the coming Messiah. This was a fulfilment of the prophecy from Isaiah 40, which is quoted in Luke 3:4-6. John has become the voice crying in the wilderness, preparing the way by declaring the message and urging all who heard it to repent of their sins and be baptised.

All sorts of people gathered to listen to John. The crowd included tax collectors, soldiers, and religious leaders, so we know that his message was reaching and impacting a wide audience. This crowd would have been familiar with the promise of the coming Messiah, and likely drawn in by John's message as he preached the declarative words of the Old Testament prophets. Furthermore, those who were present must have truly desired to hear the message since the Jordan River would not have been a close or convenient gathering spot. In many ways, this was a moment of reset for God's people. Gathering at the Jordan River—the very river they had crossed to enter into the land—marked a return to the beginning, both physically and spiritually. This particular detail brings the people full-circle as they return to this significant location for renewal and look towards their coming hope and restoration.

John's role was to prepare the people for the arrival of the Lord by way of preaching, but also through the practice of water baptism. Washing by immersion was symbolic of spiritual cleansing; an act of renewal that would have been very familiar to the people from the temple practices outlined in the book of Leviticus. Those who participated recognised that they were in need of a kind of spiritual reset in order for their lives to bear good fruit (vv.7-9). Through this, we are reminded that if we want to bear the kind of fruit that is in keeping with repentance, we must first be cleansed.

The crowd asks John how this 'bearing of fruit' can take place. Their hearts are moved and they respond to John's words, "What then should we do?" (v.10), to which John speaks to the issue of generosity and dealing rightly with others. Their receptiveness is evident as we read that the people were "filled with expectation" and even began to wonder if John was, in fact, this Messiah (v.15). He corrected them by continuing to point to the One to come, who is mightier and who will bring a baptism unlike any other (v. 16).

Preparing the way for Jesus required the renewal and cleansing of the people's hearts. This passage urges a level of introspective thought: Although the people knew the Messiah was coming, and waited in hopeful anticipation for His arrival, there were still steps they needed to take in order to prepare the way for His return. The state of their hearts and lives were important in being able to recognise and respond to their Saviour. The same is true for us. We no longer wait for the arrival of our Messiah; He has already come. Yet in the same way that John prepared the people to receive Him, let us also prepare our own hearts for the indwelling of His presence and the outworking of the good fruit that true faith bears.

Are you in need of renewal? Invite the Lord to search you and to examine your heart—to reveal anything in your life that is offensive to Him (Psalm 139:23-24). After you have confessed and repented of what He has shown you, give thanks for His cleansing and restorative work in your life.

DAY SIX

AIMÉE WALKER

Luke 3:21-38

At the age of twelve, I embarked on a project to trace my family tree. I tracked down names and birthdates and combed through old photographs my grandparents had held on to in my quest to put faces to those who had gone before me. I only made it back to my maternal great, great, great grandmother before I lost motivation and moved on to a new endeavour.

These days, it's likely that not many of us can trace our heritage back more than a few generations, but in ancient times, knowing one's lineage was essential. It was the means by which you could legitimise your claim to land or even a throne. This is why as Jesus begins His public ministry, Luke wants to make sure that we are left with no doubt that He is the One whom John the Baptist spoke of—the One who will "baptise [them] with the Holy Spirit and with fire" (Luke 3:16). He wants us to be sure that He is the long-awaited Messiah. To do this, he clearly and unequivocally establishes Christ's sonship not only through His genealogy, but also through the affirmation of the Father.

Having been baptised, Jesus is standing in the water, praying, when, in a beautiful display of unity, the Father and Holy Spirit join Him for this pivotal moment. The Father claims Jesus as His own, declaring: "You are my Son, whom I love; with you I am well pleased" (v. 22). The audible equivalent of the visible glory cloud that had travelled with Israel, this is both a declaration of the Father's delight in His son and a proclamation of His deity. Jesus is no demi-god; He is fully divine. And yet, He is also fully human.

Following strict Jewish protocol, Luke begins to trace Jesus's lineage. To the modern reader, this genealogy appears to read as though it is Joseph's—Luke's audience, however, would have immediately known that this is His mother's side of the family tree. It was Jewish custom to not directly name women in a genealogy—a practice Matthew radically disregards in his account—but to instead refer to them by their husband's name, relying on grammatical structure to identify whose family line it is. In the original language, every name is preceded by a definite article—except for Joseph. This omission signals that it is in fact, Mary's family line that Luke is recording for us, and he does so because of the Old Testament prophecies that the Messiah would come from the seed of woman (Genesis 3:15) and be born of a virgin (Isaiah 7:14). Luke chooses to establish Christ's sonship through Mary because it is essential to the legitimacy of His claim to be the Messiah.

He also chooses to follow another Jewish custom for the same reason. Jewish genealogies didn't typically skip any names—every generation was represented—and unlike Matthew, who also rejected this practice, Luke adheres to this rule. In doing so, he continues to make clear that Jesus is the One they have been waiting for, both a *son of David* and a *son of Abraham,* He is the One who will fulfil and satisfy the requirements of the Davidic and Abrahamic covenants. The One who has rightful claim to both the land *and* the throne. But the lineage of Christ has some surprises for us: This is a genealogy where firstborns are set aside. It is Seth, not Cain; Enoch, not Lamech; Shem, not Japheth or Ham; Isaac, not Ishmael; Jacob, not Esau; Nathan, and not Solomon. . . In one breath, Luke is confirming Jesus' identity and showing us that God will not allow man's faithlessness to thwart His plans; that He is willing to override custom and what we elevate to ensure His purposes prevail.

Luke's genealogy further differentiates itself from Matthew's in that he chooses to go all the way back to the very beginning, once and for all establishing Jesus' humanity and His deity: Jesus is both the *son of Adam* and the *son of God.* With His identity as the son of God bookending our passage, Luke's objective is achieved: We can be certain of the things that we have been taught (Luke 1:4). He has left no room for doubt, Jesus fulfils the human lineage that was required of the Messiah, and, in His deity, has the power to do all that was prophesied of the Messiah. And the great hope we now have, is that our lineage has been joined to His and His heritage has become ours. In Christ, we have been grafted into a family line that stretches into eternity and brings the Father great delight. Hallelujah!

How does Christ's lineage encourage you and give you confidence about the certainty of what we believe? Allow yourself to sit with the wonder and privilege of being grafted into a family line that continues to impact eternity and to consider how the Father might be inviting you to partner with His purposes for your generation.

DAY SEVEN
New Level, New Devil
AMBER PALMER

Luke 4:1-30

Years ago, when I was new to studying God's Word, I remember hearing the phrase, "new level, new devil." At the time, I was puzzled by what this was referring to. The more I studied Scripture and began to experience adversity in my own faith, I quickly learned there is an enemy dead set on distracting me from God and His purpose for my life. Although we may face intense warfare, the more we grow in our faith and in our relationship with God, the more we can trust He is faithful in equipping us to fight back against our adversary's persistent tactics.

Luke 4 shows us that no one is immune from the devil's feeble schemes to lure God's children towards sin and coveting the world—not even Jesus. Just as He steps into His public ministry (new level, new devil), we see the enemy *attempt* to thwart Jesus from His purpose. I am quite sure Satan thought he was going to be on the winning team. Dripping with deceitfulness and slithering towards a hungry and thirsty Jesus, the enemy strikes not once, but multiple times.

In this showdown we don't see swords and arrows being used to fight. Both opponents' choice of weapon are words which they wield towards one another. Utilising the classic tactic he has chosen since the garden with Eve, the devil draws on God's Word but adds his own twist. He takes the verses out of context, shifts meaning, creates doubt, and makes promises he can't fulfil. Despite the fact that Jesus is depleted of earthly food and drink, He is full of God's Word and spars back with verses from Deuteronomy:

Man shall not live by bread alone (8:3).

You shall worship the Lord your God, and him only shall you serve (6:13).

You shall not put the Lord your God to the test (4:16).

Jesus doesn't aggressively fight back with His fists to prove Himself or His purpose. He doesn't fall for the enemy's fake promises or bend to his pressure. Instead, words that were given to Moses and the Israelites long before this specific moment become the perfect comeback response when Satan hits Jesus with the law. In a beautifully orchestrated moment, the Word of God Himself confidently repeats the Word of God, putting the devil in his place with the truth.

God knows we face daily spiritual battles against the enemy who entices us with worldly things and desires. He likes to stroke our heart's worth with cravings for fancy job titles, large bank accounts, prettier homes, more invitations from friends, and expensive cars. He dangles the carrot, leading us away from wholehearted devotion for the Lord. If he can make us believe God is not enough, he wins the battle.

In Ephesians 6:10-17, Paul writes that the battles we face are not against flesh and blood but against evil spiritual forces in the heavenly realm. We must defend ourselves against the devil's attacks with the armour of God. Verse 17 specifically mentions we are to take "the sword of the Spirit, which is the word of God." Just like Jesus was armoured with Holy Spirit and God's Word, we can be as well!

The enemy is persistent and predictable but he will never prevail in our lives! God tells us that no weapon formed against us will succeed (Isaiah 54:17 NASB). Although this message was delivered by the prophet Isaiah to Jerusalem, I believe this truth can be applied today as we deal with our own spiritual battles. Even when the enemy throws his fiery darts, we know in the end his attempts will fail. God is sovereign over us. His plans are for us, to prosper us, and give us hope and a future (Jeremiah 29:11).

Both Jesus' personal example and Paul's encouragement to the Ephesians teach us the importance of relying on the Spirit and battling back with God's Word. Standing strong in the truth and speaking it out loud will send the enemy fleeing. God did not leave Jesus alone to fight the enemy and He doesn't leave us alone either. He is in it with us!

Which promises of God do you need to wield and stand firm on today? Pray the verses aloud, write them out where you'll see them, and commit to using the truth of God's Word as your weapon of warfare.

DAY EIGHT
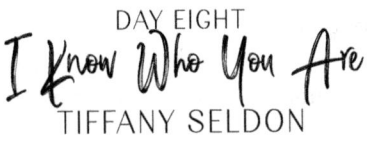
TIFFANY SELDON

Luke 4:31-44

Jesus has just been rejected in a place where He should have been welcomed. Not only was He rejected, but His life was also threatened as he was chased out of Nazareth. Now if it was me, I likely would have retreated, maybe even hidden out for a while. But this isn't the way of Jesus. Despite facing rejection, Jesus never plays into what outsiders say about Him. He has not forgotten who He is or why He came. Instead, He continues His mission to "proclaim the good news of the Kingdom of God" (v.43).

He goes down to Capernaum and begins teaching in the synagogue (v.31). The response here could not be more different than the one He received in Nazareth. The people in the synagogue marvel at His teachings, and a man with a demonic spirit begins proclaiming His identity saying, "I know who you are—the Holy One of God" (v.34). At this, Jesus commands the demon to be silent and come out of the man, and it obeys.

Jesus shuts down the proclamations of the demonic spirit even though they were true. *Why?* Jesus' mission to free the oppressed (Luke 4:18) has not wavered despite the response from those around Him. Having a demon identify you as the Messiah is unlikely to result in freedom or belief for anyone. So, Jesus casts the demon out, delivering the man from this oppression.

The result is that people now marvel at Jesus' authority and power (v.36), and the news begins to spread about Him. He continues moving throughout the area, healing the sick and demon possessed and fulfilling the prophecy from Isaiah that got Him in trouble in Nazareth (Luke 4:18-19).

After Jesus ministers throughout the region, He retreats to a deserted place (v.42). My tendency when things are good is to want to stay in the moment. I can struggle to stop and be filled by God and, instead, end up working out of my own strength. In contrast, Jesus often follows instances of ministry 'success' with solitude. He models for us the essential rhythms of renewal that exist in our relationship with the Father.

The crowds search for Jesus and ask Him not to leave. It would have been easy for Him to stay where things were good, but Jesus doesn't camp out in His comfort zone. He knows the importance of bringing the good news to other towns so that they too might hear and believe. I, on the other hand, like to stay where the people agree with me—where things are going well. I often mistake comfort in my work with God blessing my work. When I step back and put on the mind of Christ, however, I am convinced that God will call us to hard things so that more people might be set free.

As you journey on your walk with Jesus, what is your response to opposition? Does your confidence waver when you face rejection? Paul writes in 1 Corinthians 3:7-9: "So neither the one who plants nor the one who waters is anything, but only God, who makes things grow. The one who plants and the one who waters have one purpose, and they will each be rewarded according to their own labour. For we are co-workers in God's service; you are God's field, God's building."

Regardless of the responses you might face in your ministry, may your heart be encouraged that you are a co-labourer with Christ, and you have a purpose in God's redeeming work here on earth. Jesus says, "Daughter, I know who you are. I am equipping you for the good works I have prepared for you in advance. Your job is to follow me."

Consider your positioning in this season. Is there anywhere that you are trying to stay but God is asking you to go? Or that you are wanting to leave but God is calling you to stay? Ask Him to give you the courage you need to be obedient to follow Him and thank Him that He will equip you for the task.

DAY NINE
Abandoning Self-Sufficiency
SHELLEY JOHNSON

Luke 5:1-32

I can be curled up in a chair under a blanket, coughing and struggling to breathe, and still debate with myself whether or not I should go to the doctor. One part of me stubbornly argues that I'm not sick but overcome with symptoms of my ongoing asthma. But another contends, "You're sick. You need a doctor." Eventually, I admit my need for help and pick up the phone to make an appointment.

A similar deliberation consumes my mind when I refuse to admit my spiritual insufficiencies. Some kind of bullheadedness deep inside me digs in its heels, telling me that I don't require help, that I don't need Jesus' strength. Pride pushes me towards independence, and self-righteousness gloats, *I've got this!* Four men in today's passage from Luke 5, however, demonstrate for us what it looks like to abandon such self-sufficiency and embrace the All Sufficient One.

The first, Simon Peter, is a man who consistently illustrates the 'I've got this' attitude, rarely admitting his hubris and lack (John 6:16-21; Matthew 16:22). But on the day Jesus stands before him, Peter confronts his shortcomings. As a lifelong fisherman, Peter knows nets like his are not thrown into the deep during the heat of the day. However, at Jesus' command to do so, Peter reluctantly yet respectfully obeys (Luke 5:5). When his nets fill to overflowing, Peter succumbs to an overwhelming awareness of his unworthiness, humbly bowing before Jesus saying, "Go away from me, Lord; I am a sinful man" (v.8). In a moment, all his pride vanishes, and Peter admits the truth.

In contrast, the leper and paralytic come into the presence of Jesus acutely aware of their weaknesses. As outcasts in their society, these men cannot work to support themselves, so their entire existence depends on the generosity of others. The desperate leper throws himself at the feet of the One who can help (v.12), and the humble paralytic relies on friends to lay him before the Healer (v.18). Because both of these men bring their needs into the light, Jesus does not hesitate to make them whole (vv.13,24).

Finally, Levi the tax collector, who, like Peter, has lived a self-reliant and self-confident existence thus far, surprises everyone by leaving his wealth behind to follow Jesus. In his exuberance, Levi hosts a banquet for Jesus, the disciples, and his marginalised friends (vv.28-29), a sure sign his once sanctimonious heart has been changed.

In case the stories of these four men who surrender all pretension to bow before Jesus are not enough to convince us of what righteous living looks like, the Pharisees step into the narrative. Confused by the disciples' willingness to have a meal with such untouchables, the Pharisees push back (v.30), ironically demonstrating what *self-righteousness* looks like. These pious Pharisees, who embody the 'I've got this' approach to life, miss the invitation of Jesus completely while the tax collectors and outcasts accept it. Unlike the Pharisees, the people around the table know what they need to be made holy—Jesus.

Jesus' response to the doubting Pharisees, "I have not come to call the righteous, but sinners to repentance" (v.32), becomes a defining moment in His ministry. For the short time that Jesus walks the earth to preach the Good News to the poor, proclaim freedom for the prisoners, heal the blind and sick, and release the oppressed (Luke 4:18), He seeks to find the *sick*, the ones who know they require a physician (Luke 5:31). In other words, Jesus goes out to all those who are aware of their need of Him.

When we get swept up in our own illusion of self-sufficiency, we hold back on giving our full selves to Jesus because we stubbornly believe we don't require assistance—we think we should be able to do everything in our own strength. But Jesus stands before us with open arms, inviting us to lay down pride and to throw out our nets, waiting for us to admit our sickness and call to the only Doctor who can give us strength to do *all* things (Philippians 4:13).

Admitting our weakness allows us to access God's strength. Where do you need to lay down your pride and humbly ask for Jesus to be your All Sufficient One?

DAY TEN
It's in the Stretch
JENNA MARIE MASTERS

Luke 5:33-6:16

Standing in front of the chapel, I prayed silently as I looked out at a sea of middle-school girls. *How was I supposed to talk to them about who they were in Christ when, just a week before, Holy Spirit told me I needed to reset my whole identity?* In some areas, my faith was bearing healthy fruit, but this was not one of them. Instead, I had dry branches, like a "shrivelled hand" needing restoration (Luke 5:8). I believed God and His promises in relation to my marriage, parenting, writing, and our adoption journey. If someone spoke ill of me or called into question God's call on my life, however, I crumbled. I was bearing rotten fruit when it came to believing God about who He said I was. My personal identity was all shrivelled up, and I continued to hide it even when I attended church.

I'm not the first person to need restoration. In this passage, we're told Jesus meets a man on the Sabbath with a shrivelled hand (Luke 6:6). The word 'shrivelled' in Greek is *xeros*, meaning withered and dry. Strong's Concordance defines it as 'members of the body deprived of their natural juices, shrunk, wasted, withered'. When Jesus, the source of Living Water (John 4:10), sees the man's hand is literally dried up, He commands him to stand in front of everyone and stretch it out.

This man's miracle came in the stretching. I wonder if it hurt, willing his tight skin to unfold, or if he was ashamed to stand with his broken body at the front of the Synagogue. We're not told, but I felt this way when I stood up and shared with that group of thirteen-year-old girls that I was forty-three and *still* struggling with my identity in Christ. It was hard to expose my dried-up hand, but my miracle came in the stretching, too.

As I spoke that day, Holy Spirit revealed that I was the same age as these teenagers when I started to believe Satan's lies about my identity. Jesus had asked me to deliver a message on identity to preach to *myself*. As I read Psalm 139:13 to the girls: "For you created my inmost being; you knit me together in my mother's womb," I sensed His Spirit knitting me back together, restoring me to His original design, even before the earth's foundations. Just like the man that encountered Jesus, I was "completely restored" (Luke 6:10).

The Greek language describes this miracle as "restored whole," the root of which is *auxanō*, a verb that means 'to cause to grow or increase'. When we trust God with our brokenness, we are not just restored but He also empowers our faith to grow, and the miracle remains active. We create space for His power and presence to increase in our lives. It's grace upon grace, miracle upon miracle.

Have you been completely restored? Perhaps you've given yourself to Jesus Christ, but still hide a hand of shrivelled faith behind your back? You come to church, and just like the man in this passage, you wait for an invitation to stand up and reach out to Jesus.

Friend, *this* is your invitation. Jesus is waiting for you—and not just at church. He's in your bedroom, kitchen, workplace, or car, and in this very moment, invites you to stretch out the dry, parched area of your life and offer it to Him. I know it may be painful, but just as Jesus asked a paralysed man, "Do you want to be made well?" (John 5:6), it's time for you to take action and "Get up and stand"(Luke 6:8).

What areas of stretching have you been resisting? As you consider what action God might be asking you to take, surrender your weakness to the Lord and ask Holy Spirit to embolden and equip you to step out in faith today.

DAY ELEVEN

The Unshakeable Kingdom
MAZHAR KEFALI

Luke 6:17-49

We are living in ever-changing and often uncertain times, yet this should come as no surprise. In Hebrews 12 we are told that everything that can be shaken, will be shaken, but we are also told that the Kingdom we belong to is unshakeable (vv.27-29). However, key to experiencing this stability is the depths of the foundations that we lay. A truth Jesus makes clear in Luke 6 where He teaches us what is required in order to build a life that will not be shaken or collapse when the storms inevitably come (v.48).

In verses 46-48, Jesus reveals that being a follower of Him is evidenced by a life that does not merely pay lip service to calling Him Lord, but reveals His Lordship and authority by obeying His Word. The preceding verse reveals the nature and values of His Kingdom and what it means to live as subjects of the King. It begins with a recognition of our spiritual poverty before God (v.20), which should then result in a deep hunger for His ways (v.21). As we follow Him, we must also accept that the culture around us will reject us, just as they rejected Him (vv.22-23). Jesus never hides anything in the fine print. The cost is made clear up front.

As we face rejection for our beliefs, Jesus turns things upside down in terms of how we are to respond, as opposed to how we would like to. We are to forgive, turn the other cheek, give and lend to those who are our enemies, and do good to and for them (vvs.27-36). All of this reflects the character of Christ. He is not asking of us anything that He Himself did not do (Acts 10:38; Luke 23:34; 1 Peter 2:21-23).

How we respond to those who oppose what we believe and who we are as Christ followers reveals whether or not we are reflecting the heart of our Heavenly Father (vv.35-36) and the very nature of Jesus. The Father relates to those who hate His ways and His children with mercy. Jesus incarnate was the very embodiment of mercy. If we only show love, forgiveness, and kindness to those who show us the same, then Jesus makes it clear we are no different to the rest of the world.

In a sense, Jesus summarises the values of His Kingdom, the heart of the Father, and the nature of being a disciple in a simple, but defining statement: "The student is not above the teacher, but everyone who is fully trained will be like their teacher" (v.40).

It is important to note that this idea of discipleship—being fully formed into the likeness of Christ—involves not only our relationship and response to the Word of God but also to human mentoring. In the culture of Jesus' day, the discipleship of boys who could one day become a rabbi, or teacher, consisted of three distinct stages:

Bet Sefer (house of the Book): From the age of five to twelve, boys would commence reading and writing the Torah as they learned to understand the Scriptures. As these years came to an end, they entered into adulthood, as far as the community was concerned, through the celebration of their Bar-mitzvah.

Bet Midrash (house of study): From the age of thirteen to fifteen, gifted boys would go a stage further and study the remainder of the TaNaK (the Hebrew Bible—the Old Testament). Only the 'best of the best' would continue in this stage, the rest would take up a trade.

Bet Talmid (house of learning): From fifteen years onward, boys would be chosen by a Rabbi to be 'fully trained' by them in order to become a Rabbi themselves at the age of thirty.

Interestingly this is when Jesus began His ministry (Luke 3:21-23). These students were known as *talmidim*, which in Hebrew is translated as 'disciple'. Their desire was 'to walk in the dust of the Rabbi' and observe how he loved God and lived out the Scriptures. In this level of relationship, the student chose to surrender and subordinate their lives to their teacher.

As His disciples, seeking to grow unshakeable roots in an ever-changing world, may we, too, accept this challenging call to discipleship to 'walk in the dust of Rabbi Jesus', reflecting His Kingdom values, and becoming dedicated students of His Word.

Take stock of your 'foundations'. Is there anywhere that disobedience is threatening the stability of what God wants to build in and through you? Ask Holy Spirit to help you realign with the truth of God's Word and keep in step with Him.

DAY TWELVE

Jesus Draws Near
HEATHER CARLISLE

Luke 7:1-35

I should be better at this! It's a thought that often hits me when I'm surprised by yet another failure to meet the high standards I have set for myself. When you view your life through this lens of failure, you can even subconsciously think, *Who would even want to be with me right now?* I know I have. When I became a mom, between the body changes and a baby that never stopped crying, I did not feel very beautiful or successful. And yet, in the middle of feeling like a mess, Jesus came to me. His love seems to be drawn like a magnet to us in our weakness, embracing us even when we feel our most unlovable.

In Luke 7 we see the same Jesus in action. Interrupted by a crowd asking Him to heal a centurion's servant, He agrees to go, only to be stopped by the centurion himself expressing his unworthiness to have Jesus come under *his* roof. *Rabbis don't have time for Gentiles, only Jews,* he thinks. And yet, he hopes that if the rumours about Jesus are true, just maybe the miracle could extend to him. He opens his heart and, revealing his faith in Jesus' power and authority, his servant is healed. The faith in this man's heart right in the middle of his perceived unworthiness was irresistible to the grace of God. The same is true for us. God sees through all the societal rules, pressures, and expectations, straight to our heart. He sees the seed of faith even when we don't see it in ourselves.

But He also sees the places where faith has died—and even this doesn't stop Him from drawing near.

When Jesus comes across a funeral procession for a widow's only son, God's heart in the flesh breaks wide open. Verse 13 says, "When the Lord saw her, his heart went out to her and he said, 'Don't cry.'" Even our tears have purpose when it comes to our Saviour. He notices our suffering and is moved to action. In this case, Jesus' compassion compels Him to risk breaking rules for the sake of love. While Jews were commanded to stay away from dead bodies at all cost lest they become unclean, Jesus moves with decided passion directly to the casket. He even touches it. *Do you know God still burns to come to the darkest, deadened places in our hearts and lives and touch them?* He sees the ones our friends and family don't have energy for anymore. He doesn't care how ugly or how lonely those places have been. In fact, He can't be kept apart from us in our heaviest pain and grief. When we let Jesus in and let Him touch that which was once dead, His resurrection life can't help but flow into us.

This passage closes with John the Baptist hearing about these events from his prison cell. From a place of pain, doubts can sneak in, and he is beginning to question if Jesus really is the One they had been waiting for. Jesus gives him the most solid answer He can to stand on—the Word of God in the form of prophecies about Him in Scripture. And when John's messengers leave, He brags on John to the crowd. In response to hearing John's biggest doubts, Jesus calls out the gold He sees in his heart. Right when it looks like John is being swayed, Jesus affirms he is not a reed swayed by the wind (v.24), that he is, in fact, the greatest man alive—with the exception of those that are least in the kingdom of God (v.28). The heart of God is always for us, even in the middle of our doubt.

Jesus sees our heart today, and no matter how we feel about ourselves, His grace can't be stopped from coming to us. The One who is driven by love instead of obligation or cultural expectations is reaching out to us today, showing up with resurrection life, compassion, and encouragement in the very places that feel most unworthy. As He is moved to action, expect Him to change everything, and be prepared for His love to pour through you too, to reach the hearts of the forgotten, the broken, and the discouraged everywhere you go.

Where have you let doubt about God's love for you creep in? Bring those doubts to the Father and ask Him to fill you afresh with His rule-breaking love and show you what He sees. As you let Him in, pay attention to how He is reviving faith and giving you renewed expectation.

DAY THIRTEEN

TABITHA MEGLICH

Luke 7

The storm came in fast and hit hard. I was worshipping alongside my family when, without warning, that old familiar darkness enveloped me. Memories flashed like lightning, taking me back to my run-away years when I left the shelter of my Father's arms and ran headlong into the wilderness of sin. A deluge of shame and regret flooded my heart, and the weight of my past threatened to pull me under.

The pastor opened the altar. I couldn't get there fast enough. I dropped to my knees as tears began to flow. As I prayed, the Spirit led me back in time to a primitive stone-and-mortar house in a small village near Capernaum. A meal was underway, and Simon, the Pharisee hosting, was enjoying conversation with the curious Rabbi from Galilee. Onlookers crowded the room, but I was unaware of everyone but Jesus. *I was the woman weeping at His feet...*

"And behold, a woman in the city who was a sinner, when she knew that Jesus sat at the table in the Pharisee's house, brought an alabaster flask of fragrant oil..." (v.37 NKJV).

I've heard more than one sermon speak to the extravagant expense of that perfume, and that was undoubtedly the case. The flask alone, carved from marble-like stone, would have cost this woman. Yet, the price paid is not as significant as the means by which she paid it. This woman was a notorious sinner (read harlot). Perfume was her stock-in-trade—it was used to entice and was vital to her livelihood. It is reasonable to assume the fragrant oil poured on Jesus' feet that day was purchased with dirty money—earned by peddling her body.

It symbolised her descent into darkness: her loss of innocence, self-worth, and dignity in exchange for the suffocating bondage of sin. Luxuriously fragrant to others, for her it carried the aroma of guilt and shame. Her perfume was more costly than anyone in that room could have known—everyone but Jesus.

Desperate for release from the burden of her past, she "stood at His feet behind Him weeping; and she began to wash His feet with her tears, and wiped them with the hair of her head; and she kissed His feet and anointed them with the fragrant oil" (v.38 NKJV). She knew full well that ornate bottle contained only filthy rags, but it was all she had to give. As she dropped to her knees, her perfume mingled with tears—every drop, a confession.

Jesus heard the unspoken cry of her heart: *I need You. Please forgive me.*

Simon's mind was elsewhere. He had a reputation to worry about. He invited Jesus to dine, but now his guest was a spectacle. Jesus knew the thoughts of Simon's heart as well: pride, self-righteousness, and condemnation. True to form, He responds with a story: "There was a certain creditor who had two debtors. One owed five hundred denarii, and the other fifty. And when they had nothing with which to repay, he freely forgave them both. . ." (vv.41-42a NKJV).

Notice that neither creditor could make payment. Though not a notorious sinner, Simon was equally unable to satisfy his sin debt. Likewise, we are all spiritually bankrupt. Our righteousness is worthless to a perfect, holy God. But then Jesus pours out these simple words mingled with extravagant grace—words more costly than anyone in that room could have known: "Your sins are forgiven" (v.48).

Beautifully broken, the woman lays her glory at His feet, her tresses plaited and adorned just days before now tenderly caressing her Lord. The same woman who stood on the street in haughty disregard is now a living expression of humility.

Simon, the devout religious leader, did not recognise the Messiah sitting right next to him. She did. Her enraptured worship declared Him her Saviour and King.

How often do we fail to recognise Jesus in the room? Let's not take His presence—the One who paid our debt in full—in our life for granted. When we choose gratitude for the immeasurable love poured out for our ransom, and recognise the Grace seated at our table, our life is never the same.

Take some time to reflect: Where has Jesus been present unawares to you? Thank Him for His faithfulness and invite Holy Spirit to give you a heightened awareness of His presence moving forward.

DAY FOURTEEN

ADELE DEYSEL

Luke 8:1-21

An impromptu message from a friend, "Are you home? I'm on my way over!" instantly triggers in me a panic-induced cleaning frenzy. I scramble to hide the mess—shoving laundry into cupboards and dirty pots into the oven, packing the dishwasher, and vacuuming in a flash. I barricade rooms, turn off lights, and with a smile I open the front door, ashamed and flustered, trying my best to pretend everything is perfectly under control.

Shame convinces us to hide our flaws and failures, making us believe that we are unacceptable to society. We don't want anyone to see the abuse we endure, the betrayal we live with, the sorrow that suffocates us, or the addictions that we wrestle with. Our moral failures and broken marriages remain hidden in the dark. The narrative of our inadequacy and unworthiness, resulting from our mistakes, failures, and traumas, convinces us to hide our true selves to appear more socially acceptable.

Shame bullies us into isolation.

Luke 8:17 warns us that ". . .nothing is hidden that will not be disclosed, and nothing concealed that will not be known or brought out into the open." Everything hidden in the dark *will* be brought into the light. This is an intimidating promise!

The fear of rejection, judgement, and humiliation can drive us to hide the truth, but the reality is that we end up sacrificing our freedom for the opinions of others. Shame will fight to stay hidden, blinding us to the possibility of a community equipped to help us.

The heaviness we experience is often a result of our attempt to carry a burden that has already been overcome. In the beginning, God's light defeated darkness and brought order to chaos. On the cross, Jesus defeated darkness for eternity, and the enemy lost his power and hold over us. He made a way for us to step into His light and find freedom from whatever binds us.

In the parable of the hidden lamp (vv.16-18), Jesus teaches us the importance of transparency and vulnerability. Nothing is hidden from Him; He sees beyond our masks right into the depths of our hearts. His relentless, eternally unchanging love for us allows us to boldly bring our hidden shame and struggles into God's light.

1 John 1:9 reminds us that when we confess our sins, God's faithfulness will lead to our forgiveness and cleanse us from all unrighteousness. Confession breaks the chains that bind us to our shame and allows God's truth to shine a light on our next steps as we start a journey towards healing, forgiveness, and wholeness through His boundless grace.

In God's presence, shame loses its power.

We don't have to pretend to be perfect but, with honesty and humility, we can approach God knowing He will forgive, heal, and restore us. His love and grace will mend our brokenness and transform our lives. As we courageously bring our shame into the light, we embrace authenticity, openly acknowledging our flaws and frailty as we seek support and find healing within the context of community.

Consider asking God to help you find a trusted community that can journey with you and offer you support and accountability. Community in its truest form can help you erase the mistakes you have made and not highlight them. Our transformed lives can become a powerful testimony of God's redemption and goodness, and our journey the breadcrumbs for others to discover the same freedom.

Confessing our shame invites God's transformative power through grace, redeeming our failures into beauty, our brokenness into wholeness, our despair into hope, and our shame into purpose. Let's take courage in God's abundant love, mercy, and grace which are sufficient and fully available to us (2 Corinthians 12:19), knowing that the Father's love conquers *all* shame!

What sin or shame has God redeemed in your life? As you give thanks for His boundless grace, consider who might need to hear your testimony today and ask the Lord to give you opportunities to help others also step into the light.

DAY FIFTEEN

KAY GLEAVES

Luke 8:22-56

Have you ever looked back at something and felt like you were seeing it for the first time? Or maybe you finally understood how all the seemingly separate pieces connected?

That's how I felt about this passage in Luke 8. There are many stories, each offering good lessons. But when I reflected back upon it, Holy Spirit brought me new revelation, and I'm going to be honest, I wept. I wept because the Word is alive, and it ushered into my spirit a message I not only needed to hear myself, but also one I knew He wanted me to share. Maybe it will be new for you too.

Separately we read about how Jesus calmed the storm; about how Jesus restored a demon-possessed man; about all the people from the region of the Gerasenes who asked Jesus to leave; about Jarius' daughter who Jesus raised from the dead; about the woman with the 'issue of blood' who touched the hem of His garment. Each of these amazing stories is just one of many different stops in Jesus' day, and for us, a seemingly disconnected slew of incredible events from which we can glean precious insight and deeper understanding.

But what if we didn't disconnect them? I felt Holy Spirit ask. *What do you see then?*

Fear. I see so much fear.

First, we see the disciples afraid in the midst of a storm. Then, a whole legion of demons were afraid of Jesus and begging Him to cast them into pigs, rather than the Abyss of which they were also afraid. Next was the crowd in Gerasenes who witnessed all of this and were so afraid of what they saw, they just wanted Jesus to leave! Jarius was afraid he was going to lose his daughter. And the woman with the twelve-year bleeding disorder was afraid to be in a crowd, but also so afraid to stay the way she was that she reached out to Jesus and came trembling to Him when He called her out.

Fear tries to keep us untrusting. It tries to keep us stuck where we are. It shows up to confuse us and make us act out in ways that moves us further from the truth. It tells us to shut up, to stay put, and not to take chances. Fear whispers, "have no hope." It wrecks us with the belief that the danger or the cost is too great. It shames us. It lies. And if we 'bottom line' it, it keeps us from our blessings and our Kingdom impact.

But do you know what else I see? Fear flees when Jesus is encountered. Stay with that thought. It's deep.

'Encountered' means to have an experience with a person in a way that affects you or changes you. It's more than a meeting. It's more than an attentive nod. It's more than a shallow greeting. Often it's unexpected. Sometimes it's completely hoped for, other times it's simply endured. But an encounter always leaves you with a feeling of having experienced 'more' of someone and the sense that somehow both you and they are now more fully known.

So let me say it again: *Encountered.* Fear flees when Jesus is encountered.

What are you afraid of? Have you asked for an encounter with Jesus?

Afraid of dying, the disciples spoke loudly to Him. Afraid of hell, the demons begged. Afraid of what they didn't understand, the crowd chased. Afraid of losing too much, Jarius came to Jesus with his whole heart and a lump in his throat. Afraid of staying the same, the bleeding woman reached out to touch Him.

Fear flees when we encounter Jesus. He wants more than a meet up, more than a nod. He wants us to experience Him in ways that change us forever. And He's waiting for our boldness to simply ask.

Where in your life does fear have a stronghold? Carve out some time to sit with Jesus today. Be bold and ask for an encounter that will leave you forever changed.

DAY SIXTEEN

TABITHA MEGLICH

Luke 9:1-27

They were causing quite a stir—this man Jesus and that motley crew known as His disciples. The countryside of Caesarea Philippi was abuzz with reports of the miraculous works and radical teaching of this unconventional Rabbi.

They rambled from village to village like vagabonds—nothing but the shirts on their backs, confronting evil spirits, healing the sick, speaking of a new Kingdom, and lodging wherever they found a welcome mat (vv.1-6). It was a phenomenon that amazed and perplexed the people. A single question was on the mind of many: *Who is this man? He teaches spiritual things we've never heard before—and with authority! Even demons obey him!* (Mark 1:27).

None were more baffled than Herod Antipas, son of King Herod, who ruled Galilee from this capital city: "Now Herod the tetrarch heard about all that was going on. And he was perplexed because some were saying that John had been raised from the dead, others that Elijah had appeared, and still others that one of the prophets of long ago had come back to life. But Herod said, 'I beheaded John. Who, then, is this I hear such things about?' And he tried to see him" (vv.7-9).

The multitudes recognised that Jesus was no ordinary man. He was a master teacher with a substantial following who regularly took the most learned among the religious elite *to school*, and a civil radical who breached the barriers of race, ethnicity, and gender. He performed wondrous deeds—feeding five thousand from a single lunch (vv.10-17)—and empowered His disciples to do the same.

But Jesus was infinitely more.

Caesarea Philippi was in the remote borderlands of Israel; the furthest north Jesus ever took His disciples. It was rich in natural beauty, known for its wildlife and lush vegetation, and home to the highest waterfall in Israel. It was also a pagan sanctuary for idolatrous cultures from the Canaanites to Rome. The Gate of Hades, a portal to the underworld, was believed to be located here, deep within a cavern where springs fed the Jordan River.

This is the backdrop Jesus chose for one of the most pivotal conversations in Scripture—where the real story begins to unfold. As they walked through these foothills, Jesus put the question of His identity to His disciples: "Who do you say I am?" (v.20).

His disciples repeat the speculative answers they have heard from the crowds. Peter, however, offers a different response: "You are the Christ, the Son of the living God" (Matthew 16:16 ESV). Peter's words were a confession of eternal truth, revealed to him by the Spirit, that would form the bedrock of the Church.

The disciples were not the only ones listening to this conversation. Those four words—*You are the Christ*—ripped like lightning through this demonic stronghold. Jesus, the very Son of God, was standing in their midst. A confrontation that did not go unnoticed by the enemy. But just in case, Jesus made it crystal clear: "...on this rock I will build my church, and the gates of Hades will not overcome it" (Matthew 16:18).

Jesus' identity is the heart of the Gospel. His claim to be the Son of God paved the way to Calvary and is the foundation of our faith as believers.

Who do you say I am? This same question echoes through the ages. The answer matters. There is no spiritual pH paper with a range of possible answers. It is a litmus test. There is only one correct response. One true confession: "Whoever confesses that Jesus is the Son of God, God abides in him, and he in God" (1 John 4:15 ESV).

Who do you say I am? We speak the answer in our daily walk. A true disciple lives out the teaching of the Master.

Who do you say I am? The disciples abandoned everything to follow Jesus. Their lives spoke to His worthiness. *If others were to derive the answer from observing our life, who would they say Jesus is?*

Who do you say Jesus is? Do the thoughts, words, and actions in your life reflect the belief you hold? If not, ask for a fresh empowering of Holy Spirit to help you live out your faith in a way that honours and points to Jesus as the Christ.

DAY SEVENTEEN

KAY GLEAVES

Luke 9:28-62

I wasn't expecting this passage, Luke 9:28-62, to leave me with such a powerful, impactful question, but it did, and it was this: *What do my relationships look like and how are they furthering the Kingdom?*

I invite you to pause with that question for a moment and consider how our relationships with God, ourselves, and others are foundational to our Kingdom impact. It's okay if that feels heavy. It's a lot—at least it was for me.

I'll be honest, in my many years of following Jesus and reading the Bible, I've always taken each teaching, each story, as just one thing. For example, in this passage, we have the transfiguration, the healing of the boy with the unclean spirit, an argument amongst disciples about who was the greatest, and a discussion about their inability to cast out demons. We also read of a whole town who rejected Jesus and the man who wanted to come with Jesus but had a list of 'but firsts' to take care of before he could give his life to following Him. All of these are important individually, but God hasn't been working in my heart like that lately. He's been bringing new revelation by highlighting a 'theme' within the passage as a whole. It's been undoing me, and I'll be honest, this one feels particularly personal. Let me repeat the whisper Holy Spirit ushered in: *What do my relationships look like and how are they furthering the Kingdom?*

This question gave rise to many others that demanded answers, and as I sat with the passage more, I started jotting them all down. I knew they weren't solely for me, that they were for all of us so that we can have the Kingdom impact we desire. I challenge you as we walk through this passage together, to not just read these questions, but to ask them of yourselves too.

The transfiguration reminded me that our relationship with God should leave us changed—that we should look different because we have been in His presence. So I want to ask you: *What do you look like after spending time with God?* Do you encounter Him and come away better reflecting Him? Or are you more like the disciples who were "heavy with sleep" (v.32)? These questions forced me to evaluate whether I'm prone to numbing out and not making full use of my time with God.

The casting of the demon from the child took me down an unexpected road too, and I heard Holy Spirit beg the question: *What kind of relationship do you have with your own faith?* Gulp. Do I have enough faith in what He says to be true that I can walk out the commissions given to me with radical assurance? Or do I falter? But equally, am I humble? Do I allow Jesus to point out to me where my faith lacks and where I need Him more? As I pondered all of this, I was reminded that He perceives all of our thoughts and knows us intimately—even better than we know ourselves—and yet still calls us to His Kingdom work.

Further, as I observed how the disciples engaged with one another and their desire to call down fire on the Samaritans, I found myself considering how we as believers are to interact with others. We live in a time where opinions cause dismissal, and differing ideas, rifts, and we need to have determined how we will respond when others are rude to us, when they hold different opinions or are uncivil and openly dismissive. Will we stand in love and kindness and not oppose them with holy pretences offered in Jesus' name? Can we be peaceable, not 'preachable', showing others that God loves them and so do we?

The final challenge lay in Jesus' conversation with those who were walking down the road with Him. Their responses hold up a mirror for us. How important are our own relationships with Jesus? Are we willing to lay down our expectations, our hopes and dreams and plans to follow Him? Or do we have our own list of 'but firsts' that we want dealt with before we will commit to obedience? The answers will reveal whether we in fact love our own lives more than Him.

Shew. This time in the Word was fierce, and I'm still sitting with these questions. But I'm braving the answers—I hope you do too, so that together, we can further His Kingdom.

Spend some time reflecting on your relationships with God, yourself, and with others. How healthy are they currently? Where is God inviting you to grow and change so that these relationships can further the Kingdom?

DAY EIGHTEEN
Executive Assistants
EMILY TYLER

Luke 10:1-24

As an Executive Assistant (EA), I am often tasked with representing my boss as if I was her. She will send me ahead of herself to meetings, ask me to prepare documents, and instruct me to respond to requests using her voice. Having an EA is a smart business move. It allows for a greater workload and helps a business achieve its mission. As I read this passage, I can't help but think Jesus is appointing us to be His EAs!

The original word for 'appointed' came from *ana* (emphatic) and *deiknuo* (show). To be appointed in this way was a public designation for a particular task. Starting a new role and immediately being asked to act on behalf of the CEO always comes as a bit of a surprise. *Who, me? You're trusting me to carry out this task?* But we shouldn't be surprised when Jesus appoints us to go "ahead of him" (v.1) on His behalf because not only does He appoint us, but He also gives us His authority to overcome the enemy and get the job done (vv.9, 19).

In the agricultural world, when a crop is ripe and ready for harvest, you cannot delay. There is only a short window before the harvest will rot and die in the fields. Harvest time equates to workers getting out reaping, *pronto*! In the same way, Jesus tells His disciples (and now us) that there is a harvest of souls ready to be gathered. Individuals, families, and communities are ready to welcome the message that the Kingdom is near. But the EAs are few. So Jesus calls us to ask the Lord of the harvest to send out more workers (v.2). This job is for all of us.

As an EA, you care about the things that your boss cares about and the outcome of the mission. You desire your boss to be successful because their victory is also yours. *I wonder, when was the last time you prayed about the success of our Heavenly Father's mission? When was the last time you asked Him to "send out workers into his harvest field" (v.3)?*

Imagine the harvest we would see if we began to pray earnestly for the desires of Jesus' heart to be fulfilled.

One of my favourite things is a job well-done. Receiving high-fives from my boss gives me such a sense of joy and purpose knowing I'm making a positive difference. It turns out, Jesus feels the same way about the work we do for Him. When the seventy-two returned, Jesus celebrated their success as He "rejoiced" in the Spirit (v.21 ESV). This is the only time that this word is used in Scripture to describe Jesus' emotions. *Agalliaó* comes from "much, very" and "jump, leap." This is the kind of great rejoicing that leads you to jump up and down in celebration: experiential joy in its purest form. *How does it feel knowing you have the power to make Jesus rejoice by your fruitful ministry?* The work we do in the name of Jesus matters, because when we go as instructed we go *as* Jesus, and whoever listens to us, listens to Him (v.16). No wonder He's delighted in their achievement.

And yet, Jesus gives His followers a warning also. Yes, be delighted in a job well done for Jesus. But, He cautions, don't place your worth and value in what you *do* for God. Your true significance lies in "your names [being] written in heaven" (v.20). That's the real gift and joy. You are eternally loved. Some day in the future, the things that we do for Jesus as His EAs won't matter anymore, they will fall away.

So be the awesome EA, get the high-fives, obey the boss' orders, and go out equipped in His name with authority to do the work He has called and appointed you to (Ephesians 2:10). But don't forget that the real joy lies not in what you do for the Lord, but in what eternally remains: faith, hope, and love (1 Corinthians 13:13).

Where have you lost sight of the Father's mission and the authority He has entrusted you with to act on His behalf? Ask Him to recalibrate your heart and to fill you with fresh joy that in His great love, He invites you to partner with Him.

DAY NINETEEN
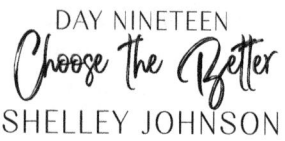
SHELLEY JOHNSON

Luke 10:25-42

In life we're constantly faced with choices. Daily, I ask myself whether to get out of bed or hit the snooze button, to put away the ice cream or have another bowl. Then, there are the spiritual decisions: *Will I sit with Scripture or scroll social media, get away for some quiet time or binge another series, pray for people or strive for control?* I want to make good choices, but sometimes I'm blind to my own assumptions or too busy or stubborn or lazy to pick the better option. So, I'm grateful Luke has taken the time here to tell stories that teach us about holy decision-making.

Our passage opens with a Jewish lawyer who asks Jesus how to have eternal life (v.25). In typical Jesus-fashion, He answers with more questions, extending the lawyer an opportunity to answer for himself. Citing Jewish law accurately, the lawyer explains one must "love the Lord your God" (Deuteronomy 6:5) and "love your neighbour" (Leviticus 19:18).

To justify his own way of thinking (Luke 10:29), the lawyer then pushes Jesus for clarification of what defines a 'neighbour'. His answer takes the form of a parable in which Jesus shocks His Jewish audience by teaching that the 'neighbour' is, in fact, the hated unclean Samaritan (v.33).

In weaving together this story and parable, Luke constructs a picture of what it looks like to resolve to *love others* intentionally. He puts the 'Good Samaritan' before us to challenge and expand on our own definition of what loving our neighbour looks like so that we can embody Jesus' greater vision.

Luke follows this dialogue with a story about Mary and Martha—an account that does not flow chronologically but thematically. Hoping to show us what it looks like to choose wisely, especially when it comes to our faith, Luke uses the two sisters' responses to Jesus as an illustration of what it looks like to *love God* well.

At the home of His friends, Jesus continues instructing His disciples. Sitting at His feet, Mary takes in every word her Rabbi speaks while Martha busies herself with preparations to the point of distraction. Frustrated because her sister is not doing her "duty," she complains to Jesus. Much like the lawyer, Martha questions Jesus in order to justify her actions (v.40).

Jesus' reply to Martha becomes a word of warning for us. We, too, can get "worried and upset about many things" when only one thing is needed—time in Jesus' presence (vv.41-42). In other words, we can become distracted by our own agendas and miss the greater good Jesus has for us. We can get wound-up so tightly with all our busyness that we fail to choose "what is better" (v.42).

While presenting these contrasting responses to Jesus and our neighbours, Luke highlights how holy decision-making intermingles with God's brand of love. Love is commitment—it is making up our minds to do what is right, no matter how we feel (1 Corinthians 13:5). Love becomes our motivation so that unlike the priest, the Levite, or Martha, *what we do* does not become our god. Each time we determine to live out our faith from the outflow of our love for God (James 2:14-26), we react to each situation more like Mary and the Samaritan.

Distractions abound, and they make decision-making all the more difficult. But, Luke has given us a template for responding to life in healthier, holier ways. Rather than allowing our assumptions or lengthy to-do lists to dictate how we conduct ourselves, we can let our love for Jesus empower us to choose what is better. In doing so, our motivations and decisions will spill out of that love, splashing onto others as we move about in the world.

Where have you become worried and upset recently? What would it look like to lay down that agenda and instead be motivated by love?

DAY TWENTY

Teach Us To Pray
TIFFANY SELDON

Luke 11:1-28

Imagine you've been following Jesus for some time now, and there He goes again, withdrawing to be alone to pray. Perhaps it didn't make sense at first, maybe it even felt counterproductive at times to stop forward momentum for this time of solitude. But as time has passed, you have seen the power that proceeds from this time alone. You now know that prayer is not only essential for Jesus, but you want to experience this type of prayer for yourself. As Jesus returns, you ask Him, "Lord, teach [me] to pray" (v.1).

Jesus follows with a simple and relatively short prayer, but each line illuminates a posture of His heart as He talks to the Creator. In this section of Luke, we see Jesus setting the stage for a prayer life that is essential, powerful, and beautifully relational.

First, Jesus teaches us to address God as "Father." It may be common practice today but this was not the case for the Jews of that time. In fact, the Jews wanted to kill Jesus for "calling God his own Father, [and] making himself equal with God" (John 5:18). In doing this, Jesus is inviting us to address God with the intimacy and love of a personal relationship. Think about the relationship between a parent and a child. There is very little parents wouldn't do for their children. In calling God "Father," then, we embrace the perfect parenthood of our Heavenly Father who delights in talking with His children.

While Jesus highlights the personal nature of God as our Heavenly Father, He also holds Him as holy and set apart (v.2). His intentions towards us are good and His love for us is perfect. From this perspective, we can trust that He knows and will do what is best for His children, even when we don't understand it.

After recognising God as set apart, Jesus instructs us to focus our prayer on His purposes with the words, "Your kingdom come" (v.2). This is an invitation for us to participate in bringing God's Kingdom to earth as we examine what opportunities He has set before us to do the will of God in the here and now.

As we partner with God in this way, It can be easy to find ourselves working 'for God' while still relying on our own strength. Jesus teaches us to remember our dependence by bringing each need to our Father (v.3). Because He is a good Father, God delights in giving us more than we could ask or imagine (Ephesians 3:20). Even when what we need might just be enough energy to get through the day, we can be encouraged that God sees us and knows how to give good gifts to us, His children (vv.11-13).

This acknowledgement of our physical dependence is followed by a reminder of spiritual dependence (v.4). It offers a moment to reflect upon the forgiveness our Father graciously offers to those who ask, and also prompts us to extend this same forgiveness to those that have wronged us. Though this may be difficult at times, the forgiveness required from us is minor in comparison to the grace and mercy we each have received.

Jesus closes out this prayer with a request for protection. This isn't an ask for physical protection as one might expect from an itinerant preacher, but rather protection for our hearts that can so easily go astray. Only through His help can we be delivered from temptation, and when we inevitably fail, we can have confidence in His forgiveness and compassion towards us.

Following this prayer template, Jesus offers encouragement that we can approach God with boldness in prayer confident that when we ask, He *will* respond (v.9). However, it is not our boldness that makes our prayer effective but the kindness of God that allows us to draw near, and that same kindness that desires to answer and give us what we need.

As we look at our prayer life, may we do so knowing that we have a kind Father who wants to talk with us, providing everything we need as we follow Him.

Where do you need Jesus to breathe fresh life into your prayer practice? Talk to your Father and ask Him to do a new thing in your prayer life.

DAY TWENTY-ONE

God-Blessed Eyes
EMILY TYLER

Luke 11:29-54

Have you ever wished that you could see Jesus perform His miracles right in front of you? I know I have, so to hear Jesus reprimand the crowd in this passage so vehemently for asking for a sign can feel quite affronting. Yet, part of the reason He does so is because He already *was* right in front of them.

Jesus uses the examples of Jonah and the Queen of Sheba to make His point. The Ninevites—a wholly depraved "city of bloodshed" (Nahum 3:1 NRSV)—responded to an unwilling messenger and repented.

The Queen of Sheba, a pagan woman no less, sought God with great tenacity and was prepared to travel from "the ends of the earth" (v.31) to encounter Him. In both cases, the Ninevites and the Queen of Sheba accepted messages from God's fallen, broken, and flawed emissaries. And here, we see those who considered themselves enlightened rejecting the Light of the World and asking Him for proof!

Despite their exposure to the light, this generation of everyday, normal people like you and me blame Jesus for their lack of faith. He responds by telling them that their lack of spiritual sight is not from a lack of light but faulty eyesight. If you consider glaucoma, cataracts, or other vision-related diseases, the verdict is the same: Seeing clearly isn't about how brightly a light is shining, it all comes down to the health of your eye.

Jesus warns us that if we have unhealthy eyes then we're at risk of our whole lives being "full of darkness" (v.34). As the Light of the World (John 8:12), Jesus is the One who illuminates and reveals the Father (John 14:7). But there is an enemy who does not want us to recognise His light. Paul tells us that, "The god of this age has blinded the minds of unbelievers, so that they cannot see the light of the gospel that displays the glory of Christ, who is the image of God" (2 Corinthians 4:4). If our eyes are like windows allowing light into a room so we can see clearly, it's as though Satan has been chain-smoking for decades, dirtying, discolouring, and staining the windows to make them incapable of letting in the light.

In verse 33, Jesus says the purpose of lighting a lamp is so that others "may see." The original word used here, *blépō* can be translated as 'seeing something physical, with spiritual results'. Jesus wants us to have 20:20 spiritual eyesight—a perception and discernment that leads to understanding the truth of who He is—and tells us *we* have a responsibility to make sure we're seeing clearly (vv.35-36)!

Lighting a lamp in Jesus' day was akin to trying to start a campfire with a piece of flint. There was no switch to flick, and it took time and effort. No one would labour to light a lamp and then hide it. Just as the function of lighting a lamp is to illuminate, bring clarity, and reveal the environment in which it's placed, the function of the eye is to receive that light. When your eye is healthy then your whole body benefits.

It can feel overwhelming to know the responsibility for ensuring "the light within is not darkness" (v.35) is ours. And yet, the good news is that when we come to Christ, our spiritual eyes are opened. Ephesians 5:8 tells us that we once *were* darkness but now we are "light in the Lord."

If you're struggling to see clearly, tell Jesus what it is you can see. When the blind man initially saw people "like trees walking around" (Mark 8:24) he didn't have full clarity. But Jesus didn't leave him this way. He went to work until the man could see "everything clearly" (Mark 8:25)—and He will do the same for our spiritual eyesight, too.

God doesn't want us asking for signs because He's already right in front of us. Rather, He wants us to ask for greater *sight*. And spiritual insight is a gift He's already given (Matthew 13:11-17 MSG). Jesus wants to turn on your light (Psalm 18:28 TLB) and give you "God-blessed eyes—eyes that see!" (Matthew 13:16 MSG)—we only need to ask!

List the areas where you're struggling to understand or see God's hand at work. Bring your list before the Lord and ask Him to give you 20:20 spiritual eyesight to perceive how He is moving in your life.

DAY TWENTY-TWO

No Reason to Fear
PAULA MORRISON

Luke 12:1-34

Even though it can be hard to find the right words sometimes, I have found that simply telling people not to worry about their future concerns is rarely helpful. As a child I used to always say, "Don't worry Mum, I will be fine" before rushing out the door because I knew she was worried for my safety. As a mother, I have tried to reassure my children not to worry about upcoming exams or events at school as God is with them. As a wife, it has been a revelation to be married to someone who genuinely never seems to worry but, in reality, everyone worries about something. We all have things that keep us awake at night or are on our minds when we first wake up.

In this chapter, Jesus is speaking to His disciples about various contexts that lead to worry and how important it is to put things into perspective. Knowing that all of them except John would ultimately die for their faith, Jesus first addresses worry in relation to persecution (vv.4-11). Having witnessed the recent opposition to Jesus, the disciples are understandably anxious. However, Jesus wants them to know that if they publicly acknowledge Him now, He will, in turn, acknowledge them before the throne of God. Since God holds ultimate power over life and death, honouring and obeying *Him* needed to be their primary concern rather than worrying about those who might persecute them.

I love how Jesus comforts and reassures the disciples that their life is valuable and worth more than many sparrows. When we are being persecuted, it is tempting to feel worthless and forgotten, but here Jesus teaches that a loving God *values* His disciples. If God knows how many hairs are on our heads, we can trust He knows everything about us and our situations. In moments of great testing, the disciples could trust that Holy Spirit would speak through them even if they felt unprepared. We, too, can be confident that Jesus promises spiritual strength and guidance for those who testify of their faith in Him during times of persecution.

Later in the chapter, Jesus tells the disciples not to worry about their physical needs—what they will eat, drink or wear—because life is about so much more and they have eternal matters to pursue (vv.22-34). Essentially, the lesson here is that if we seek first the kingdom of God, our worry will be replaced with a greater concern for God's Kingdom. When we worry about material things, we are forgetting our value before God and how much He loves and cares for us. If He provides for the birds, after all, we can trust God will provide for our needs, too.

Interestingly, in the middle of Jesus' teaching, a man interrupts to ask a question about an inheritance dispute with his brother (vv.13-22). Jesus goes on to tell a parable about a successful farmer who plans to store his surplus grain so he can take life easy, eat, drink, and be merry. *If we are honest, don't we envy this rich man who has his future all mapped out? After all, who doesn't want earthly success and future security?* Yet, here Jesus is teaching that trusting in earthly riches instead of acknowledging that everything we have comes from God is foolish. True wisdom is understanding that He is the source of all the blessings in our life, and He deserves our heart's highest affection.

When worries keep you awake at night or distract you during the day, look at the birds and remember that you are a dearly loved child worth more than many sparrows. As the flock of God (v.32), we can trust in the Good Shepherd's provision and care, and with the power of the Spirit to face all that is ahead, we truly have no reason to fear.

Where do you need to be reminded that you are worth more than many sparrows? What does it look like for you to trust God in that place and seek first His Kingdom?

DAY TWENTY-THREE

Dressed and Ready
VICKI BENTLEY

Luke 12:35-59

My daughter is counting down the days until her sixth birthday. Every morning, she eagerly runs to the calendar and crosses off another square, her anticipation growing. She wants to be sure that when this special day finally arrives, she—and everyone else in the family—will be fully prepared and ready to celebrate!

Scripture tells us we should be "eagerly waiting for [Jesus] to return as our Saviour" (Philippians 3:20 NLT). But while this will be a day of great celebration for all believers, it's far harder to anticipate an unmarked date on the calendar, one that is known only to the Lord (Matthew 24:36). *How are we supposed to maintain a state of excited readiness when we don't know how long we are supposed to wait?*

It is precisely this question that Jesus speaks to in this passage of Luke. Like a servant guarding his master's house, we are to "be dressed ready for service. . . so that when he comes and knocks [we] can immediately open the door for him" (Luke 12:35-36). In other words, we must remain in a constant state of readiness and avoid falling into the trap of complacency or allowing our attention and affections to wander elsewhere.

When Moses met with God on Mt. Sinai, the Israelites grew so tired of waiting for his return down the mountain that they turned to idol worship. We read in Exodus 32:1, "When the people saw that Moses was so long in coming down from the mountain, they gathered around Aaron and said, 'Come, make us gods who will go before us. As for this fellow Moses who brought us up out of Egypt, we don't know what has happened to him.'"

With the benefit of hindsight, we might shake our heads at the fickle nature of the Israelites when, time after time, Moses had proven himself to be a trustworthy leader and God had remained ever faithful. Yet, living out our Christian witness amid the suffering, hopelessness, and hostility of a broken world can take a toll on our resolve too. We may find that our hope and anticipation for our Saviour's triumphant return can fade with time as our love for Him that once burned so brightly grows cold.

This heart change can also be reflected in our behaviour. While we may not be concerning ourselves with the construction of a golden calf, perhaps we are inadvertently bowing to little gods of our own making as the source of our ultimate hope. We may not be going so far as "beating the other servants, partying, and getting drunk" (v.45 NLT), but maybe we aren't treating the precious gifts God has entrusted us to steward on this side of heaven with the care and respect they deserve.

Without a set date to look forward to, it's easy to fall into the trap of thinking we have all the time in the world to prepare, but verse 45 reminds us we must "be ready, because the Son of Man will come at an hour when you do not expect him." Like a thief, He will break into the carefully constructed life we have built for ourselves and deliver the judgement our unfaithful hearts deserve (v.46). In contrast, "If the master returns and finds that the servant has done a good job, there will be a reward" (v.43). Our faithful diligence, our perseverance in the waiting, will not go unnoticed. And this should give us all the motivation we need to faithfully continue doing the work He has called us to do as an offering of devotion to our Master in heaven (Colossians 3:23).

Jesus said in Revelation 22:7, "I am coming soon!" We may not know how soon, but we can be sure a day of glorious celebration awaits. So, let's live out each day with a spirit of ready anticipation and follow this advice from 1 John 2:28, "And now, children, stay with Christ. Live deeply in Christ. Then we'll be ready for him when he appears, ready to receive him with open arms, with no cause for red-faced guilt or lame excuses when he arrives"

Where in your life is the desire and ability to be faithful waning? Ask Holy Spirit to give you a deeper revelation of and renewed expectation for the return of Christ. How does what He's showing you spur you to continue to do the work He has entrusted to you?

DAY TWENTY-FOUR
True Friends
REBEKAH BERMINGHAM

Luke 13

Recently I wasn't invited to a wedding, and I'm not going to lie. . . it kinda threw me. You see, the couple and I played netball together, we were both in the same life group, and the rest of my friend circle had been invited. I felt like. . . *What!? How could you not have invited me?* I was disappointed because, well, I thought we *knew* each other!

But then I began to ask myself, *Would I have invited them to my wedding?* And as I thought about it deeper, I realised, no, I wouldn't have. Even though we both participated in the same activities, they hadn't journeyed with me through the breakup or job difficulties I had been facing; they had simply offered a passing prayer. When John, the husband, was sick with glandular fever, I wasn't able to sit with him in his hospital room because I only found out about it through his wife's Instagram feed. It turns out, actually knowing someone and being known by them as opposed to just occupying the same spaces or sharing the same beliefs are two entirely different things.

In Luke 13:22-30, Jesus teaches about the narrow door to God's Kingdom and how many who think they *know* God and will be invited into His Kingdom, don't really know Him at all. Luke writes, "Work hard to enter the narrow door to God's kingdom, for many will try to enter but will fail. When the master of the house has locked the door, it will be too late. . . You will say, 'But we ate and drank with you, and you taught in our streets.' And he will reply, 'I tell you, I don't know you or where you come from'" (vv.24-27 NLT).

Now that might seem a little harsh, but the chapter opens with the title "A Call to Repentance," and woven throughout are demonstrations of God's love, along with a call to closeness, to friendship—to *truly knowing* God. It's a reminder that God is an intimate, jealous God. He didn't just stay in heaven and wish this sinful world well; He came down, in person—divinity wore the muck and grime of humanity—to reconcile us to Him. In verse 10, we see Him going against all social constructs and norms to heal a woman on the Sabbath even though He knew that it would make him an enemy of the religious elite, and it is these men, in fact, who later prove that while they know God's laws, they don't actually know His heart. So when Jesus is talking about the narrow door, it's not due to a lack of love or care but too much of it! It shows us that Jesus has a burning desire for true relationship and genuine friendship with us—the ones He died for!

Hebrews 12:6 reminds us that, "The Lord disciplines those He loves" (NLT), but that starts with repentance—a willingness on our part to surrender our thoughts, hearts, and lives to His leading. While we might see a call to repentance as a picture of punishment or distance, God sees it as the beginning of true friendship and relationship with Him. Hebrews 12 continues: ". . .Only irresponsible parents leave children to fend for themselves. Would you prefer an irresponsible God? We respect our own parents for training and not spoiling us, so why not embrace God's training so we can truly live?. . . God is doing what is best for us, training us to live God's holy best. . . It's the well-trained who find themselves mature in their relationship with God" (Hebrews 12:8-11 MSG).

God does not draw our attention to sin to shame us, but to transform us, so if the Lord is highlighting something to you right now, remember that heeding His instruction and repenting is a beautiful thing. It is the beginning of a friendship with a God who adores you and the doorway to His Kingdom. We cannot obtain this intimacy without an obedient and surrendered heart, just like we cannot have a wedding invite without a deep relationship developed through nitty gritty conversations and long nights spent at that metaphorical hospital bedside.

If we always desire the reward of intimacy without the refinement of discipline and repentance, we'll never become true friends who *know* our Father's heart, just acquaintances who miss out on the real wedding banquet with our God. So open up your heart and heed His call. . . Both to repentance and that roast dinner final feast.

Is there any way in which you have got trapped in the motions and religious cycles of faith or allowed sin to create distance between you and God? Take some time to repent and return to a place of intimacy through renewed surrender and obedience.

DAY TWENTY-FIVE
Table Talk
TABITHA MEGLICH

Luke 14

Right there, in the middle of their living room, sat my sister-in-law's weaving loom. It was an anniversary gift from my brother and the fulfilment of a dream for her. The tall chest of drawers in my bedroom still displays an exquisite linen dresser scarf crafted by her hand.

The art of tapestry begins with stretching warp threads across the loom to create a cohesive foundation. The consistency of these threads lends the tapestry structure and integrity while weaving in the weft threads adds colour and texture to the design. Jesus was a master weaver too—of truth, that is. Throughout His ministry, He revealed the mysteries of the Kingdom of God through a tapestry of parables, each adding spiritual hues to this eternal story.

In Luke 14, Jesus attends Sabbath dinner with a group of religious leaders, an invitation that involves more than it appears. This Pharisee and his cohort intend to put Jesus on exhibition in hopes of finding fault with Him. Little do they realise the guest at their table is the omniscient One who knows their thoughts and peers into their hearts. As they break bread, Jesus tells six seemingly distinct parables. Looking closer, we see the Storyteller masterfully using the theme of 'invitation' as the common thread by which He weaves five Kingdom truths:

Humility First (vv.1-11): Observing the guests vying for prominent positions at the table, Jesus makes it clear that the emptying of self is the essence of greatness in the Kingdom. This parable echoes His comments about the Pharisees coveting the uppermost seats in the synagogue just days earlier (Luke 11:43).

Pure Motives (vv.12-14): Knowing the covert nature of His host's invitation, Jesus hits the issue head-on, teaching that purity of heart calls for generosity with no expectation of return. Whereas His host invited Jesus to glorify Himself, Kingdom culture embraces *the least of these* for the sake of love (Matthew 25:40).

By Invitation (vv.15-24): This parable teaches that not all who are invited will enter the Kingdom. With nuances of the *Parable of the Sower* (Matthew 13:1-9), Jesus warns that temporal concerns—financial security, daily tasks, and relationships—will cause many to decline the invitation to sup with the King of Kings.

There is a Cost (vv.25-33): This parable is an invitation to genuine discipleship. Composed of two complementary halves, Jesus tells a cautionary tale of embarking on an endeavour without proper preparation. Through it, Jesus reveals that He has not come to draw the masses, but those who have considered the cost and accept the invitation to "follow" regardless: "And whoever does not carry their cross and follow me cannot be my disciple" (v.27).

The twelve could not have known then that walking in the Way would eventually cost them their lives. But they did understand when Jesus called out, "follow me," He was asking them to walk away from the life they knew towards a new life they did not yet understand. The implication was this: *Following Me is going to cost you.* Yes, accepting Jesus as Saviour is the easy part. Surrendering to His Lordship is the journey of a lifetime.

No Turning Back (vv.34-35): The full stop to Jesus' table talk that day was a solemn warning: Kingdom impact requires perseverance in faith and good works. We must continue to walk in righteousness because as Jesus cautions us, "Salt is good, but if it loses its saltiness, how can it be made salty again? It is fit neither for the soil nor for the manure pile; it is thrown out" (vv.34-35a).

In reading this passage of Scripture, I was captivated by the thought of sitting at Jesus' feet, listening to Him speak of His Kingdom—a Kingdom where humility reigns, hearts are made pure, and lofty and lowly alike are cherished and loved unconditionally. The Kingdom He purchased with His life.

Jesus is worthy of our life and love, no matter the cost. And when we choose to follow Him, our life is woven by His grace into the eternal tapestry—the incomprehensibly beautiful Redemption Story.

Of the five Kingdom truths outlined here, which do you sense God is inviting you into at a deeper level? How can you accept that invitation and what does it look like to outwork it in your life?

DAY TWENTY-SIX

Lost and Found
PAULA MORRISON

Luke 15

A few years ago, I was in San Francisco with a friend. We had booked a trip across the Golden Gate Strait, and the plan was to catch the 10am ferry. It was a beautiful day and we enjoyed our time strolling along until suddenly, around 9.55am, we both looked at each other and came to our senses, realising we were not where we needed to be! Having walked completely in the opposite direction, we had missed the ferry and were now lost! Fast forward to this year: I was visiting a local address but as hard as I tried, I couldn't find the house. I finally had to call for directions and when I arrived, I realised the GPS had taken me to the back of their property concealed by a high hedge. I was so close but still lost!

The truth is, you can be lost no matter your proximity to home.

The familiar parable of the Lost Son powerfully illustrates this for us. Despite its title, it is actually a story of *two* brothers whose contrasting behaviour offered distinct lessons for Jesus' audience. We are told at the beginning of the chapter that the story of the younger son was for the benefit of "the tax collectors and sinners" listening to Jesus, while the story of the older son was for the Pharisees and the teachers of the law (vv.1-2).

In this parable, Jesus radically redefines sin and salvation for His audience. The younger son demonstrates the traditional idea of sin—wild living, insulting his father, and being self-indulgent. However, the older brother's sinful motives are reflected in his moral conformity—he does what is expected culturally of him, works hard, and does all the right things in order to obtain a successful life. However, even though one son behaves very badly and the other obeys his father to the letter, neither was focused on their relationship with their father; they both wanted the father's things, but not *him*. Instead they used him to get what they wanted: good times, wealth, and status. And while one lived a 'moral' life and the other an immoral one, the reality is that both sons were lost, and both needed to be reconciled to their father.

Who do you relate to? The younger son valued independence and sought personal happiness through enjoying the good things of life and following his passions wherever they led him. *How is that working for you? Is it time to come to your senses?* No matter your past mistakes, because of the person and work of Christ on the Cross, our Heavenly Father responds to you 'coming home' just like the father in the parable—filled with compassion running to his son, throwing his arms around him, and kissing him. He even puts the best robe on him and gives him a ring with the family seal on it, a sign his father was restoring him fully as his son. What a picture of the grace of God this parable gives us!

Perhaps you relate more to the older brother. *Is life not going well even though you are trying to do everything right?* It is easy to look at others and think, *I deserve more as I behave better*. However, God offers us an identity that must be received, not achieved by good works. First and foremost, He has called us to be His child; He doesn't look at us according to our achievements but as one who is found in His Son. We need, therefore, to lay our good works at His feet and stand in His righteousness alone.

Just like both sons in this parable, the lostness we often feel is due to loving the wrong things. Our soul belongs to God and everything we value in this world is a gift from Him. He alone deserves our highest allegiance and He alone can satisfy our souls. Only by loving the Father and abiding in Him will we find our way to where we truly belong: in the Father's house.

Which brother do you most relate to in this story? Why is this? Invite Holy Spirit to reveal any lies that you have been believing about your relationship with the Father and thank Him that His arms and house are always open to you.

DAY TWENTY-SEVEN
Wise Wealth
VICTORIA STEWART MALONE

Luke 16

My maiden name is Stewart. In researching my ancestry, I learned that this name comes from the occupational title, *Steward*. The *Royal High Stewards of Scotland* managed the entire country, and this office was the most powerful position next to the king. Over time, the Stewards adopted the hereditary title as their surname.

A steward was paramount in overseeing the king's possessions. His role encompassed handling the daily operations of his Lordship's home and properties, supervising the staff, and conducting political and business affairs. The steward bore the responsibility of managing the use of his king's wealth, which was a position of immense trust and commitment. The master's kingdom growth was based on the steward's wise use of his wealth.

In Luke 16, Jesus uses two parables to teach about wealth and the proper place it should have in our lives. He first tells His disciples about a dishonest but shrewd steward who acts to benefit his own interests over his master's. The second parable tells of a rich man living a luxurious life who ignores the needs of a poor, dying man at his own front gate.

These parables highlight examples of the unwise use of wealth. We have heard the saying, "Money is the root of all evil." Scripture clarifies the truth behind this saying and instructs, "For the *love* of money is the root of all kinds of evil. And some people, craving money, have wandered from the true faith and pierced themselves with many sorrows" (1 Timothy 6:10 NLT). Jesus's straight talk about worldly wealth tells us, "No one can serve two masters. Either you will hate the one and love the other, or you will be devoted to the one and despise the other. You cannot serve both God and money" (Luke 16:13 NIV).

Money is neither good nor evil, righteous or unrighteous; it is a tool that can measure our faith in God's provision, our love for Jesus, and our concern for others. As faithful stewards, we wisely use our wealth to align with God's values, prioritising love, compassion, and generosity over selfishness.

I don't often think of myself as a steward, even though my family name should remind me daily! Yet Deuteronomy 8:18 commands, "But remember the Lord your God, for it is he who gives you the ability to produce wealth." Wow! What a reality check! I am a Royal High Steward to the King of Kings, and so are you! *Will we choose to be dishonest or wise stewards?*

Are we practising wise wealth when we consistently spend too much on takeout rather than cooking a meal and sharing it with the young, single mother next door? Are we like the dishonest steward when we justify buying another pair of shoes for our ever-growing closet collection, but 'can't afford' to give to those in need? Are we robbing God (Malachi 3:8) when we hold tight to our wealth, benefitting ourselves instead of our Master and His Kingdom?

In 1 Chronicles 29:11-18 (NLT), King David prays a beautiful prayer that reveals his love for God rather than money. *Can we pray this prayer, devoting ourselves to being faithful stewards of King Jesus?*

> "Everything in the heavens and on earth is yours, O LORD, and this is your kingdom. We adore you as the one who is over all things. Wealth and honour come from you alone . . . But who [are we] that we could give anything to you? Everything we have has come from you, and we give you only what you first gave us!. . . It all belongs to you! I know, my God, that you examine our hearts and rejoice when you find integrity there. . . [Help us] offer [our] gifts willingly and joyously. . . Make [us] always want to obey you. See to it that [our] love for you never changes."

When God examines our hearts may He find integrity there.

To which master are you devoted: Jesus or money? What needs to change for your love for Jesus to reflect wise handling of wealth? Humbly ask the Lord to transform you into a generous and joyful steward.

DAY TWENTY-EIGHT
Unlimited Forgiveness
DAN TYLER

Luke 17

Commentaries won't get you very far with Luke 17. It's variously described as a patchwork, having no discernible theme, and being beyond study. This is in part because while we have Jesus' responses to people's questions, the questions themselves aren't always recorded for us. In the first place, we have Jesus teaching that God loves His people so much that He will protect them from things that cause them to stumble (v.2). And that protection means that the person who brings the stumbling block will be treated as an enemy of God. It is a fearful warning.

But how should we respond to those who are bringing us stumbling blocks? Well, says Jesus, we should rebuke them and then forgive them. We should tell them that they're wrong and then, if they repent, give them a second chance. Obviously we must forgive everyone if we want to experience the full power of God's forgiveness towards us. Think of the line in the Lord's Prayer, "forgive us our sins, as we forgive those who sin against us" (Luke 11:4 NLT). But this contingent forgiveness—"I forgive you when you say sorry"—is a hint to the nature of the stumbling blocks in verse 1. They are the things that make coming back to God difficult.

I recall a colleague who runs a church for those on the streets. When someone takes his support and wastes it, he rebukes them, and when they repent, he offers his support again. It's not that he refuses to offer support to those who don't repent, it's that they have to come back to the source to receive support—and in coming back to the source they are enacting a kind of repentance.

As C.S. Lewis says: "Repentance is not something God demands of you before He will take you back and which He could let you off if He chose; it is simply a description of what going back is like."

So how often does God do that for us? There is no limit. But are we really expected to offer unlimited forgiveness to others? I can't even do it seven times! I don't have the faith for that. It's no wonder the disciples cry out, "increase our faith!" (v.5).

Jesus' reply is huge. Even the tiniest faith in a God like ours can do more than you would ever believe possible. *Do you have a forgiveness challenge in your life?* You have all the resources of heaven on your side—even if you just *want* to want to go there... But even if you don't feel like forgiving, it doesn't matter. You still have to practise forgiveness. Seek the good of those who oppress you. That's what Jesus says—and that's exactly what He does.

In the next story, we see Jesus running into ten men who need His pity (vv.11-17). Their leprosy puts them in a lower social class than an illegal immigrant or escaped convict. In fact, if you want to carry the same emotional weight in our culture, the contemporary equivalent to a leprous Samaritan would be the way we think of a sex offender or convicted slave trader.

Is Jesus really going to practise what He preaches? Is He really going to offer forgiveness and healing to them? Yes. Yet only one comes back to thank Him. *Really? Didn't they realise how much it cost Jesus to offer them a fresh start?*

When we set out to live like Jesus—even offering grace and forgiveness to a Samaritan leper—it feels like an impossible task. Forgiving others at this level costs more than we can possibly afford. So we find ourselves crying out: "This is too much for me!" Especially when we receive no thanks or recognition. In this context, Jesus teaches us something about the way the end will come (vv.20-37). We do not understand it. We will not be able to predict the time or manner of the end. But when it comes, we want to find ourselves fully given to the work of forgiveness.

We can't take grudges with us, so any thought of the next world will begin the cathartic work of right-sizing our unforgiveness. In fact, the more we meditate on God's plan for us beyond this life, the more we will be able to extend forgiveness. The more we extend forgiveness the more we will become "good and faithful servants." And the better we serve Him, the more useful we will be to others—especially those closest to us!

Is there anyone whom you are holding a grudge against or are unwilling to forgive? Come before the Lord today and confess your unforgiveness. Receive His grace and ask Him to empower you to give yourself fully to the work of forgiveness as you declare your trust in His ability to bring healing to your heart.

DAY TWENTY-NINE
Upside Down
SHELLEY JOHNSTON

Luke 18:1-34

The popular Netflix series *Stranger Things* captivates audiences with its imagined happenings in Hawkins, a quiet town in Indiana. Just out of sight is a parallel dimension, a separate yet connected world called the "Upside Down." Little by little, the creatures from this other world turn Hawkins topsy-turvy, causing confusion where there was once comfort and taking what was once known and tossing it on its head.

In a not-so-similar fashion, Jesus steps across dimensions to usher in a new Kingdom on earth—a new way of living and thinking. Everything the Jews thought they understood about faithfulness, Jesus turns upside-down—widows are elevated over wealthy, tax collectors are justified more than Pharisees, and children lead the way into the Kingdom of God.

Each of the stories Jesus tells in today's passage paints a picture of contrasts in order to highlight what faithful living looks like under the new covenant of Christ. And, it starts with prayer.

In a world where a judge would be respected and trusted and a widow ignored and pitied, Jesus flips the script, demonstrating the way of God's Kingdom and the power of persistent prayer. The uncaring, selfish judge serves as a foil for God, who is not only trustworthy but responds to all requests with justice (Luke 18:7). The marginalised widow shocks Jesus' listeners by her tenacity, teaching us all how to put our faith into practice.

Pharisees were held in high esteem in first century Israel because they consistently followed the law and did everything that was required—like fasting twice weekly and giving a tithe (v.12). In great contrast, Jewish tax collectors, viewed as traitors, were despised and distrusted universally. Jesus juxtaposes these two men as they pray: the Pharisee proud and self-righteous, the tax collector humble and repentant. Jesus changes the game by telling His audience it was the tax collector who "went home justified before God" (v.14). In God's Kingdom, a faithful life is sourced by humble prayers.

Yet humble prayers are but a step towards right-living. As children come to Jesus, full of innocence and joyful acceptance, their reception of Him stands in stark contrast to the sceptical Pharisees (Luke 5:21, 20:2). Children in this ancient culture held no status, so Jesus lauding them as *the standard* for receiving the Kingdom of God would have been a shocking reversal of their accepted role in society. The humility embodied by children sets the mould for Kingdom entry (v.17).

Jews of Jesus' day would have viewed wealth as a sign of God's favour and blessing. So, when Jesus asks the rich ruler to sell everything and give it to the poor, a seismic shift would have been felt by all. The greater lesson in this story teaches us how to step away from anything that has a hold on our hearts more than God—and few things grip harder than a love of money (1 Timothy 6:10). Jesus knows this man of wealth has some letting go to do before he can enter God's Kingdom (Luke 18:24).

Throughout His ministry, Jesus uses metaphor, parable, and juxtaposition to help His followers envision the Kingdom of God. Elevating the prayers of the widow and taxpayer over those of the Pharisee as the epitome of faithfulness shatters assumptions and makes room for a better understanding of God's heart. Challenging cultural norms by saying children more easily enter God's Kingdom than wealthy rulers turns the Jewish world upside-down.

Much like first century Israel, our current culture holds tightly to its own values and ideals. And, like Jesus' followers, we are at risk of pursuing the world's ways of elevating those who look the part and have the power. But, if we are to live faithfully for God's Kingdom, we must allow Jesus' comfort-shattering ways to flip our assumptions and habits, moving us towards persistent prayers, humility, and surrender. Just as He once told Israel, "I desire steadfast love and not sacrifice" (Hosea 6:6 NRSV), God still does not desire showy striving or worldly success—just the simple faithfulness of our unpretentious hearts.

Praise God that His ways are higher than our ways and ask Him to show you where you have inadvertently transposed culture onto what it means to be faithful. Invite Holy Spirit to help you step into the fullness of living life the topsy-turvy Kingdom way.

DAY THIRTY

Again and Again and Again

EMILY TYLER

Luke 18:35-19:27

At just a little under 1.5m in height, I've always felt a deep connection with Zacchaeus. You know that eccentric short woman you might spot at the supermarket, climbing the shelves to retrieve that essential ingredient for her dish because, let's face it, without it, the whole dessert just won't come together? Well, that's me. But after spending time in today's passage, I hope I can be like Zacchaeus in many more ways than simply sharing our short stature.

Blind beggar Bartimaeus (Mark 10:46) and Zacchaeus' stories are the last two reported incidents prior to Jesus entering Jerusalem. These two individuals, despite their stark differences in socioeconomic status, share striking similarities. Bartimaeus, impoverished and destitute, and Zacchaeus, possessing wealth and influence, find themselves equally despised by society and cast out. Yet both men possess an acute awareness of Jesus' presence as He passes by, and both are impeded by the surrounding crowd. Nevertheless, fuelled by an unyielding determination, they refuse to let this opportunity slip away.

Bartimaeus calls out. He shouts, and is rebuked by the crowd, but this just fuels his desire to shout "all the more" (v.39). Jesus responds to his efforts and, after Bartimaeus' verbal proclamation that Jesus is in fact "Lord" (v.41), he receives his sight.

Zacchaeus on the other hand is a chief tax collector—first in rank, he would have had a team of other tax collectors working under his purview. Known for swindling and stealing (Luke 3:13), tax collectors were widely despised by the Jews. This didn't stop Zacchaeus for he wanted to see *who Jesus was* (19:3); he wanted to know the essence of this man he'd heard about. Driven by unwavering determination, he was prepared to employ any means necessary to discover the secret ingredient of this man they called Jesus.

Running ahead to climb a tree might seem like no big deal to us but it was utterly incongruous of a man of Zaccheaus' status to run, let alone climb a tree. These are the actions of a desperate man, a man filled with zeal. Jesus invites Zacchaeus to "hurry and come down" (v.5 ESV). Sensing the urgency of the moment, for the second time Zacchaeus acts promptly and presents himself before Jesus, seizing the opportunity for a life-changing encounter.

The culmination of these two narratives is encapsulated in verse 10 where Jesus' mission is made clear: He came to seek and save the lost. Yet Jesus is not the only one doing the seeking. Just as He was not far from these two unseeing men, He is close to us too, and it is His desire that like them we would "seek God, and perhaps feel [our] way toward him and find him" (Acts 17:27 ESV). *So, what are you willing to do to seek Him? What measures are you prepared to take to gain a clearer view of Jesus? Are you ready to cry out, to change position, to hasten with urgency, or perhaps even run towards Jesus?*

Like the crowds, there will always be barriers to reaching Jesus, but we must persevere. Maybe we need to risk being laughed at, ridiculed, misunderstood, ignored, shut out, gossiped about (19:7), or rebuked and silenced (18:39) to meet with Jesus. But if we take that risk, we see from Bartimaeus and Zacchaeus that our lives will be forever changed.

My favourite word in this passage is *zéteó*, the original Greek for 'seeking' in 19:3. To *zéteó* is 'to give priority to, purposefully pursuing, attentively searching for, and making diligent efforts to find by any means'. But what I love most about the use of *zéteó* is that in this verse Luke uses the vivid imperfect tense which makes the seeking relentless: Zacchaeus seeks Jesus again and again and again.

Friends, we are to *zéteó* Jesus. For He desires to enter our homes and lives, too. Don't let Him pass by and miss out on the opportunity to respond quickly to His call *today* (Hebrews 4:7).

While many of us might relate to Zacchaeus in sharing a limited viewpoint of the world, I hope we will, with unwavering resolve, embark on a lifelong journey of seeking first Jesus and His Kingdom: again, and again, and again.

Get honest about your current level of desire to pursue Jesus. Identify the things that are obscuring your vision and consider what you need to do in order to gain a clearer view of Jesus. Ask Holy Spirit to make you willing and to enable you to persevere. Thank God that He promises to be found by those who seek Him.

DAY THIRTY-ONE

MARISSA PRICE

Luke 19:28-48

In what feels like an abrupt pivot from the first half of chapter nineteen, verse twenty-eight transitions us to a very significant event: In a moment of sober anticipation, Jesus rides into Jerusalem, not as the conquering king many had anticipated, but humbly and with the promise of a different kind of deliverance.

As He nears Jerusalem, Jesus speaks to the people, explaining through a parable that the Kingdom of God is not going to appear at once (v.11). This was necessary as the prophets of the past had spoken of God's promise to rescue His people and of the coming King, setting expectations of the One who would rule Israel. This passage sheds light on the fact that, although the fulfilment of the promise of the Messiah is coming, or indeed has already arrived, He is not going to appear in the way the people are expecting. After sharing this parable, the passage continues to highlight one fulfilment of Scripture after another, cementing Jesus' rightful place as the King of Israel. It is against this backdrop that Jesus now continues on to Jerusalem seated on a donkey fulfilling the prophecy found in Zechariah 9:9.

Those who had been following Jesus on this journey to Jerusalem spread their cloaks on the road, an act of great respect and honour that had been carried out to announce kings in the past (2 Kings 9:13). Yet Jesus weeps, knowing all of the events that are about to take place—the people's rejection of Him and the coming destruction of Jerusalem. The Pharisees recognise this symbolism and the shouts of messianic declaration and are upset, commanding Jesus to tell the people to stop. Jesus responds, "I tell you, if they keep quiet, the stones will cry out" (v.40). His words here mirror Habakkuk 2:11, once again alluding to His Kingship.

Jesus then goes into the temple and drives out the merchants, disrupting their corrupt sacrificial systems that had become more market than ministry. His words here, "'My house will be a house of prayer'; but you have made it 'a den of robbers'" are direct quotes from Isaiah 56:7 and Jeremiah 7:11. The phrase, "den of robbers" draws attention to the injustice taking place in the very place that is meant to be dedicated to the Lord using the same words that the prophet Jeremiah had once spoken in that location when he spoke to the corruption of the leaders.

While there are several details to notice in this brief passage, the main theme here continues to be one of fulfilment. Grand statements are being made in subtle hints and references that are setting up, what feels like, the beginning of the end. Yet, the One who was to set the captives free, to overcome the power of darkness, and to bring about salvation, was not bearing a sword or accompanied by an army. He was, instead, greeted with hostility by the very ones who were waiting for the Messiah to come.

It can be difficult to reconcile that those who were waiting in hopeful anticipation for the Messiah still missed Him when He was right before their eyes. Perhaps they had lost sight. Even today, we can miss the God who reveals Himself to us, because He may not come the way expected. Or, like those in the temple, we lose sight of the goal and get mixed up in the details. Perhaps their redemption in that moment was that Jesus continued to teach in the temple daily after that moment of confrontation. Perhaps those who had just been rebuked were beginning to experience the opening of their hearts and minds to see the Messiah as He truly is and would then choose to follow Him. And perhaps our hope, too, is that as He continues to speak today, we might truly know the Messiah in our own hearts and lives, and likewise, choose to follow Him.

How can you join your voice with the "stones [that] cry out" declaring Jesus' praise? Take some time to intentionally 'spread your cloak' before Him, bringing Him the adoration and honour He is due.

DAY THIRTY-TWO

DAN TYLER

Luke 20:1-26

"Do not remove a fence until you know why it was put up in the first place."

This is a summary of the heuristic device known as Chesterton's Fence which states that no-one puts the effort into building a fence unless they have a good reason. It might be to keep a bull in a field, keep strangers out, or something else entirely. But you had better understand why the fence was built before you pull it down or you risk losing something of far greater value than a fence.

In Luke 20, we see a huge contrast between people who pull down the proverbial fence without first considering the consequences and Jesus' response to a complex question. In the parable of the tenants, Jesus describes tenants who treat servants of the landlord with cruelty, and finally kill the son of the landlord. They think that, by killing the heir, they will be able to take possession of the property. In marked contrast to their foolishness, Jesus' response to a question about paying taxes to Caesar is to "give to Caesar what belongs to Caesar, and give to God what belongs to God" (v.25 NLT).

Wisdom displays a second-order level of thinking. It says that although the Roman Empire is evil, God's calling is to honour Him and not set up our own empire to replace the Roman one. Jesus embodies this wisdom for us. He Himself was not enamoured by the machinations of the Roman Empire, and I'm sure there were plenty of people around Him who wanted to see an end to it. It would have been incredibly easy for Jesus to use this moment to start a revolution. And yet He refuses. While there are many who would recast Jesus as a revolutionary figure, depicting Him alongside prominent political activists, the truth is, He never waves a metaphorical placard about the issues of the day; He never tries to start a revolution. In fact, "My Kingdom is not of this world" is a mantra Jesus comes back to in his darkest moments.

We all feel some frustration at the way the world is. How we channel that frustration is critical. The tenants of the vineyard mixed frustration with greed and behaved in an anarchical manner. There is no silver bullet when it comes to designing the world. There is no perfect church leadership. There is no perfect structure. If you destroy something, there is no guarantee that the thing that replaces it will be any better.

Whether your church is Episcopalian, Presbyterian, Congregational, or something else entirely, someone designed it carefully. Someone put up that fence for a reason. It's unlikely that you fully understand all its nuances and complexities, not to mention all the things it is protecting you from. If you blow up the system you may well regret it later on. If you remove a dictator it's not always obvious that their replacement will be an improvement. If you leave your church, end relationships, or even switch careers, there's no guarantee your situation will improve. You may even find it makes things worse in surprising ways.

The anarchist is willing to break the law, to ruin their reputation, or to damage their family or their church because the end justifies the means. The problem is that the only One who can say that is the One who can see all the ends: God. All the consequences of your actions are not known to you. The tenants in the vineyard justified murder and abuse because they thought that the end result (owning the vineyard) justified their behaviour. While it may seem obvious to us, they couldn't see that they were being foolish.

When Jesus is challenged about the origin of His authority in verse two, the question at stake is whether Jesus has the authority to tell people how to live. Jesus showed them that they already believed His authority was from God, but they doubted it because they didn't like the implications of His teaching.

In His response to the question about taxes, Jesus claims that pulling down fences, that anarchy, is not God's plan for His people. If we believe that Jesus speaks with a heavenly authority—that He sees *all* the ends—then we, too, are called to give to Caesar what is Caesar's and to God what is God's. Especially when we don't want to.

Where is God asking you to set aside your own agenda and instead pursue the wisdom of the Kingdom? What does this look like and what concerns or frustrations do you need to entrust to the Father to be able to do this?

DAY THIRTY-THREE
The Attention of the King
HEATHER CARLISLE

Luke 20:27 – 21:4

Sometimes only God knows how much of a sacrifice it is to surrender something to Him. A few years ago, a friend of mine was in a very toxic relationship with a family member. This relative treated her terribly, and everyone could see what a strain the consistent pain and borderline abuse put on my friend's life. All of the voices of wisdom and authority in her life were telling her to draw firm boundaries, but still she struggled to let go of the relationship. She could see the impact it was having on her, but she didn't have many family members living nearby and she felt the tug to continue seeing them. Time and again, she would come to our small group at church and just cry. The burden felt unbearable, yet others had a hard time understanding why it was so hard for her to take this step of faith.

One night as I prayed for her, God brought me to the story of the widow's offering in Luke 21: "Truly I tell you," Jesus said, "this poor widow has put in more than all the others. All these people gave their gifts out of their wealth; but she out of her poverty put in all she had to live on" (vv.3-4).

I heard God so clearly say, "Tell your friend I said, 'I know what following through in obedience costs you right now... Everything." This relationship was her 'everything'. In a very hard season of life where her relationship tank was already very low, God was asking her to give up even more. My empathy for her grew as I saw the compassion in Jesus' eyes. He was watching her sacrifice her all, and He was captivated. It took so much trust in His goodness and provision that this sacrifice wouldn't leave a gaping hole in her life.

God is unimpressed when we, like the synagogue leaders of the day, only offer showy gifts that don't cost us at all. On the outside they were doing all the right things, but in secret, all the wrong ones. Jesus says in chapter 20:47, "[the teachers of the law] devour widows' houses and for a show make lengthy prayers. These men will be punished most severely." Their acts may have looked like generosity to the world, but Jesus cut through to their hearts. I love how He then chooses the very one who had been harmed by the religious elite to praise. God keeps score, and He knows how to right the wrongs in our lives. The painful, private gifts are often the ones that catch His eye.

There is no offering you have made for the Lord that hasn't moved His heart. He doesn't miss acts of sacrifice, because it reminds Him of His Son. When you, like Jesus in the garden, would rather pass the cup of suffering but still say, "yet not my will, but yours be done" (Luke 22:42), this is an eternal treasure that God will continue to admire. That time you followed through in obedience when everyone else said you didn't have to—He saw it. The time your flesh was screaming at you to lash out at someone who may have deserved it, but you brought it to the cross instead—Jesus called all the hosts of Heaven together to brag on you. When you surrendered control of the area of life you had a death grip on because it meant everything to you—it blessed His heart.

You have all the attention of the King of Heaven today as you offer small things that no one else may notice. It all matters. So, let's keep going, knowing the One who knows us best doesn't miss a thing, and He will reward us and meet our every need as our loving Shepherd.

Tell the Lord the things that you're scared to fully relinquish to Him. Ask Him to remind you of His heart for you and to meet you afresh in this place of surrender.

THIRTY-FOUR

AIMÉE WALKER

Luke 21:5-38

It was one of those seasons you'd like to hit the fast-forward button on. The country was in a recession, and as a consequence, my husband soon found himself unemployed. We were struggling financially, but that wasn't the only challenge we were facing, and it felt like almost every aspect of my life was unravelling. Fear had a firm grip on my heart until the Lord convicted me with these words from Isaiah 8:

". . .Do not fear what they fear, and do not dread it. The Lord Almighty is the one you are to regard as holy, he is the one you are to fear, he is the one you are to dread, and he will be a sanctuary. . ." (vv.12-14).

Something about these verses halted me in my tracks and caused me to redirect my fear and to instead revere the Lord, allowing Him to become bigger in my heart and mind than the things that I was facing. As I did, I experienced what Isaiah promised: God became my sanctuary, my shelter in the storm, my safe-place.

I've been grateful for this lesson for many years now. As I've navigated seasons of transition, nursed a child through mental illness, lived through a global pandemic, and now find myself in the middle of another recession, Isaiah's instructions continue to ground my life. And they're not unlike Jesus' words to His disciples in Luke 21 where He warns them of the troubles they will face as they await His return.

Jesus' attention had been on the widow who gave her all, but the disciples on the other hand were struck by the splendour of the temple and the beautiful stones that adorned it (v. 5). Instead of joining them in their admiration, Jesus begins to tell them that there will be a time "when not one stone will be left on another" and it will no longer remain (v. 6). Interestingly, the disciples don't doubt what He is telling them, they simply want to know *when* (v. 7). But Jesus never directly answers their question—in fact, Luke records for us in the opening verses of Acts that Jesus would later tell them, "It is not for you to know the times or dates the Father has set by his own authority" (Acts 1:7). Instead, He focuses their attention on *how* they are to wait for His return.

Firstly, He instructs them to not be deceived, warning them that many will become preoccupied with dates and timing, pointing to wars and revolutions as evidence that the end is *now*. But Jesus cautions the disciples that they are but a sign that the end is *near*. He also tells them that they are not to be a cause of fear for the believer but of hope; we are to "lift up [our] heads because [our] redemption is drawing near" (v. 28). Nor are wars or earthquakes or famines or even persecution to be a source of worry for the believer because we know that the Lord will give us "the words and wisdom" that we need, and that as we stand firm we gain the life that really matters—*His* life.

In this passage, Jesus addresses events that have now come to pass—namely the fall of Jerusalem in AD 70—as well as ones that are yet to be fulfilled. While thousands of years now separate the two, there are patterns that are important for us to understand as we navigate our own season of waiting and interpreting the signs. The first event mirrors the latter: God's judgement of Jerusalem and her fall become a picture of when God will judge the nations and evil and rebellion will be fully and finally condemned. Yet even in judgement, there is hope. We live in "the times of the Gentiles" (v.24), a time where though it appears God is slow in keeping His promise to return, He is actually exercising patience because He desires "everyone to come to repentance" (2 Peter 3:9).

Temples, wars, and famines will come and go—even Heaven and earth will pass away, Jesus tells us, but His word never will; it remains *forever* (v.33). What He has said can be trusted because *He* can be trusted. So don't allow His apparent delay to cause you to doubt or worry or fear; don't allow your heart to get weighed down (v.34), at just the right time, He will come "with power and great glory" (v.27). Until then, wait well, with your eyes and heart fixed on Him alone, allowing Him to be your abiding sanctuary.

How would you describe your own waiting? Are you preoccupied with signs and times or are you focused on serving the Lord faithfully until He returns? Bring any worries and fears you have about living in this season of history to Him and invite Holy Spirit to redirect your fear to where it belongs: In reverent worship of our returning King.

DAY THIRTY-FIVE

MAZHAR KEFALI

Luke 22:1-38

As this passage of Scripture unfolds, a conflict of characters and hearts are revealed. It is the time of the Passover, the remembrance and celebration of the miracle of God's deliverance of His people, Israel, from slavery and bondage in Egypt (Exodus 12). The Passover was also a prophetic picture of the Messiah, the sacrificial Lamb of God.

As the hour of His crucifixion draws near, Jesus institutes the Lord's Supper—the celebration of the bread, His body, and the cup, His blood. This is an act He will not participate in again until the eternal Kingdom and the marriage supper of the Lamb (vv.17-18; Revelation 19:9).

As the disciples participate in communion, still not fully understanding what is about to take place and what this new sacrament means, Jesus reveals that one of them will betray Him (vv.21-23). This throws them into a state of bewilderment and causes them to become suspicious of one another. Ultimately, the corrupt heart of Judas is revealed as he betrays Jesus and sells his soul for money to those looking to kill Him (vv.1-6).

Unbelievably, the conversation at the table then turns into a dispute concerning who is the 'greatest' among them. Perhaps this sudden turn towards self-seeking elevation is designed to throw each other off the trail concerning the identity of the betrayer. Nevertheless, at a time when Jesus is in need of their support, the disciples reveal they are still a work in progress.

Jesus uses this moment as a teaching opportunity to once again remind them that His Kingdom and ways are in sharp contrast to the ways of the culture. Greatness in God's Kingdom is not defined by position at the table, prestige, or power, but rather the willingness to humble oneself and to lead by serving, just as Jesus did (v.27). To give them a further reality check, Jesus warns them that very soon all of this will be put to the test—their faithfulness and their loyalty. What they were truly made of was about to be revealed.

Jesus starts by addressing Simon, but the original language makes it clear that this was not a private 'one to one' chat, off to the side. Even though Simon is singled out, we can tell from the plural pronouns used that everyone was included (vv.31-38). In addressing Peter, Jesus uses his old name in a repeated form: "Simon, Simon." Emphasising his name in this way conveys a sense of solemnity and of deep concern. There is also a tone of sadness along with rebuke, or warning, involved.

Jesus then informs Simon, and the rest of the disciples, that none other than Satan has made a request to "sift you like wheat" (v.31). The language is reminiscent of Satan's request of God concerning Job (see Job 1:9-12; 2:4-7). In both of these examples, we see clearly that Satan is not a free agent able to do as he pleases, especially in relation to God's people. He is a roaring lion on a leash. There are boundaries in place. God is sovereign over all, and Satan has limited powers, all subservient to the redemptive purposes of God.

Satan's request was for a specific purpose—to sift the disciples like wheat. In these times, the sifting process was carried out with the purpose of separating the grain from the chaff—removing unnecessary and unwanted elements and leaving pure grain. Figuratively it conveys the idea of being shaken by an inward agitation, separating what is desirable from what is undesirable, for the purpose of testing one's faith. Using this metaphor in this context, Jesus is revealing to the disciples what is about to occur in their lives—a violent sifting or shaking, that would soon reveal their own hearts to themselves, and also separate the impure from the pure—removing any unnecessary elements from what needed to remain in order for them to be fruitful.

This process is still vital today. For as Peter would later write in his letter to the church, it proves the genuineness of our faith and will "result in praise, glory and honour when Jesus Christ is revealed" (1 Peter 1:7). May we, like Peter did, learn to rejoice when the Lord allows us to be sifted.

Where are you currently being sifted? What do you perceive God desires to reveal to you, and how can you actively participate in this invitation? Let the lessons learned from past seasons of sifting—where God worked for your benefit and His glory—anchor you at this time.

DAY THIRTY-SIX

The Cup of Life
AMBER PALMER

Luke 22:39-65

One of my favourite things about reading the Bible is seeing how God tenderly, and with great purpose, weaves details beautifully together. It's been a sanctifying process to slow down while studying God's Word and be more in tune with noticing word repetition, meanings, and the connections between the Old and New Testament. While diving into this passage of Luke, I couldn't help but become drawn to the word 'garden'.

Sin first took place in a garden.

In the Garden of Eden, Adam and Eve walked with God in perfect harmony with a heart full of worship. It was within this very garden of *shalom* that sin first entered and rooted itself deep into every human heart. Adam and Eve felt the painful tear and distance from God as they made their way out of the garden and into a different life of labour, heartache, sin, and death.

In Luke 22:39, we find redemption in a garden.

Jesus made it a routine to visit the Garden of Gethsemane at the bottom of the Mount of Olives to pray. Near the very spot the olives went through a pressing process on heavy stone slabs to produce olive oil, Jesus experienced a similar pressing from His trajectory that awaited Him on the cross. All the times in the past, present, and future that humanity turned from God to serve selfish desires and agendas, Jesus would endure them. He knew the pain of separation from God was upon Him. On His knees in prayer and surrender, He spoke these words, "Father, if you are willing, remove this cup from me. Nevertheless, not my will, but yours, be done" (Luke 22:42 ESV).

In the Old Testament, the 'cup' was used to describe God's judgement and wrath over sin. God warned in Isaiah 51:17 that Jerusalem would drink a cup of His fury. In Jeremiah 25:15, the same cup of fury is used as a threat against those who come against Israel. Here, Jesus asks God to remove this cup that He would later gulp down on our behalf. Knowing Jesus would be the only One who could handle the fate of a sinner, God does not relent but sends an angel to strengthen Him (Luke 22:43).

If we hit pause and rewind to the Passover dinner where Jesus introduces another cup to His disciples, this powerful scene in the Garden of Gethsemane will inspire a deeper reverence. Around the table with His disciples, Jesus holds a cup not filled with wrath but, better yet, filled with a new covenant by way of His own blood that would be poured out for the forgiveness of sin.

Because God so loved the world, Jesus obediently partook of the cup of wrath so that we may drink from His cup full of grace, forgiveness, redemption, and reconciliation. He willingly took the cup of fury from our hands and exchanged it with His cup of life.

And it is this cup of life that gives us the assurance that we will spend eternity in God's presence. For just as sin began in a garden, it will also end in one:

"Then the angel showed me the river of the water of life, as clear as crystal, flowing from the throne of God and of the Lamb down the middle of the great street of the city. On each side of the river stood the tree of life, bearing twelve crops of fruit, yielding its fruit every month. And the leaves of the tree are for the healing of the nations. No longer will there be any curse. The throne of God and of the Lamb will be in the city, and his servants will serve him" (Revelation 22:1-3).

Adam and Eve left the garden of Eden with death on the horizon but Jesus came with a new covenant so that we may enter eternal life with our Heavenly Father. Death may have been the beginning of the story but it won't have the last say. May our hearts be in awe and filled with gratitude for the cup of life we have been given instead of the cup of fury we deserve. Thank You, Jesus.

Carve out some time to take communion. As you drink from the cup of life, give thanks for the Father's extravagant grace and invite Him to strengthen you for what He has asked of you and to lead you into deeper intimacy with Him.

DAY THIRTY-SEVEN
The Paradoxical King
VICTORIA STEWART MALONE

Luke 22:66-23:25

Did you watch the coronation of King Charles III? The grandeur and stateliness were almost too much for the modern imagination! His Majesty was robed in purple, the colour associated with royalty since ancient times. He wore a coat of gold as the antique diadem which graced regents before him was placed upon his head. The crown, passed down from a long lineage of monarchs, held five pounds of precious jewels set in gold. With his ermine mantle of black-spotted white fur and golden sceptre, King Charles III epitomised elegance, power, and dominion.

Amidst resounding praise, King Charles stood confidently on the balcony of Buckingham Palace to wave at crowds of devoted subjects expressing loyalty and support for the newly crowned King. Streets were packed with throngs of people just hoping to get a glimpse of the king and be a part of this legendary, once-in-a-lifetime event!

When King Jesus appears in our reading today, He is not in His own palace but that of the Roman Governor, Pilate. He is on trial, accused by the Jewish religious leaders of claiming to be the King of the Jews. Despite being the King of the Universe, His paradoxical story is nothing like that of King Charles III's.

At the heart of a paradox lies an inherent contradiction—a statement that appears to defy logic or reason. It is a proposition that requires us to hold two seemingly contradictory truths in tension, inviting us to embrace the mystery of its complexities. In the realm of faith, this paradox challenges our logical thinking and demands a shift in perspective. We read in Luke 19 that just a few days before, Jesus entered Jerusalem to adoring crowds who spread palm fronds before Him, symbolising victory and triumph. A chorus of voices rang out from those packing the streets to get a glimpse of their King on this momentous occasion: "Blessed is the king who comes in the name of the Lord!" (Luke 19:38). Like King Charles III, Jesus was given the worship and devotion due a king.

However, the idolising crowds soon turned their backs on Him when they realised He did not fit *their* picture of the political saviour who would deliver them from Roman rule. The Jewish religious leaders brought Him before Governor Pilate, seeking condemnation for His blasphemy saying, He "claims to be Messiah, a king" (Luke 23:2).

As Jesus stands on Pilate's grand balcony, mockingly adorned in a royal purple robe, Pilate does not see a Sovereign King before him, but a bloodied, beaten shell of a man incapable of posing any threat. Isaiah 53 tells us, "There was nothing beautiful or majestic about his appearance, nothing to attract us to him. He was despised and rejected—a man of sorrows, acquainted with deepest grief" (Isaiah 53:2-3 NLT). Rather than accolades, the crowds below shout accusations: "Crucify him! Crucify him!"

Here we see the embodiment of the paradoxical King, whose divine wisdom chose a path of redemption through suffering rather than station. While the coronation of King Charles III speaks of temporal authority, the crucifixion of Christ unveils the eternal authority of the divine King. Jesus chose the way of the cross—a path that seemed foolish and weak in the eyes of the world—to demonstrate the magnitude of God's love and the depths of His grace. Through His suffering, Jesus offers redemption, forgiveness, and the invitation to partake in His eternal Kingdom.

As we reflect on today's Scripture, let us contemplate the paradox of Jesus, the King of Kings, who was crucified and crowned with thorns instead of being exalted in the manner of earthly kings. Let's embrace the contradictory nature of Christ's reign, finding inspiration to live lives of humility, selflessness, and love, knowing that true glory emerges from the unexpected places where heaven and earth meet. May we lay down our crowns of worldly ambition and embrace the paradoxical path of Christ, knowing that in surrendering to Him, we find true glory and eternal life.

Does your life radiate the transformation that Jesus's Kingship brings? Or have you created a paradox by saying one thing and living out another? What does it look like for you to make Jesus the King of your life today?

THIRTY-EIGHT

VICKI BENTLEY

Luke 23:26-56

The scene is set. God's radical act of sacrificial love to reconcile His people to Himself once and for all is unfolding before our eyes (Hebrews 7:27) and, amid the clamour and chaos, in a place infamously known as "the Skull" (v.33), the spotless lamb will be slaughtered for the sins of all. "With his own blood—not the blood of goats and calves—he [will enter] the Most Holy Place once for all time and [secure] our redemption forever"

But first, He must suffer on our behalf. As we read in Isaiah 53:5, He was to be "pierced for our transgressions. . . crushed for our iniquities," His broken body taking on our punishment and providing the healing and peace humanity needs so desperately. And so, not only does He endure the sneering and the mocking and the intense physical and spiritual agony—He does it *willingly*.

Jesus says in John 10:17-18, "I lay down my life—only to take it up again. No one takes it from me, but I lay it down of my own accord." Friends, Jesus' love for us is so great that He *freely chose* to lay down His life in a manner that caused Him untold physical, emotional, and spiritual suffering. *Why?* Because He loves us.

Even in the final moments of Jesus' earthly life, His love for the people around Him trumps any desire to retaliate in kind. Too weak to even carry His own cross, He turns to the weeping women following Him and says, "Daughters of Jersualmen, do not weep for me; weep for yourselves and for your children" (v.28). Instead of railing against His treatment, shouting at the injustice of it all, His heart is filled with compassion for them and the suffering that awaits. Looking down from the cross from where He would shortly breathe His last at the scene below, there were no threats or words of condemnation on His lips for the people behaving abominably— only a prayer: "Father, forgive them, for they do not know what they are doing" (v.34). And when the guilty criminal who had earlier reviled Him asks to be remembered, Jesus offers Him mercy saying, "Truly, I tell you, today you will be with me in paradise" (v.42-43).

In these acts of selfless love, Jesus escalates the challenge He set to us in John 15:12-13 to, "Love each other as I have loved you. There is no greater love than to lay down one's life for one's friends" (NLT). This is what loving like Jesus looks like—offering compassion, forgiveness, mercy, and grace, and perhaps even our very lives, to those who do not deserve it, and may even reject it. It is a weighty responsibility indeed, but thankfully God knows our limitations and "has given us the Holy Spirit to fill our hearts with his love" so that we can love as He does (Romans 5:5 NLT).

When the crowd witnessed the death of Jesus, they "went home in deep sorrow" (v.48 NLT), while the centurion recognised they had "killed the righteous one" (v.47). But their realisation had come too late, and now they had only regret. As witnesses to these events through God's Word, we, too, must decide how we will respond. The criminals hanging beside Jesus offer us a clear comparison. *Will we confess our unworthiness and our need for a Saviour or will we continue to doubt and belittle Him, questioning who He is and what He can do for us?* (v.39-40). Only one of those ways leads to life.

"For God so loved the world that he gave his one and only Son, that whoever believes in him shall not perish but have eternal life" (John 3:16). This life is ours to claim because of the Saviour who laid His down. Let's respond by worshipping Him with the honour and glory He deserves, sharing the life-giving hope we have received with those who have yet to experience the compassionate, merciful, and outrageous love of God.

Who is God inviting you to demonstrate His love to at this time? What does this practically look like? Ask the Father to soften and prepare their hearts to receive Him and to fill your own afresh with His love so that you can freely minister to them.

THIRTY-NINE
Polishing the Prophecies
MAZHAR KEFALI

Luke 24:1-35

Death is an unnatural state. It was never intended by God to be part of life, but as a consequence of sin, death became a reality for all humankind. When it strikes, it creates a sense of disorder, pain, and grief. This is the case for the first followers of Christ as they come to terms both with His death and the unexpected events of the resurrection.

The first people on the scene at the tomb are a group of women who have come to anoint the body of Jesus with spices. This very act indicates that they, along with the other disciples, have no anticipation of finding a risen Christ. Upon their arrival, they find the stone rolled away and encounter angelic beings who remind them of what Jesus had already told them would happen. They utter the words that changed the course of His followers' lives and, also, of history: "Why do you look for the living among the dead? He is not here, he has risen! Remember how he told you, while he was still with you in Galilee: 'The Son of Man must be delivered into the hands of sinners, be crucified and on the third day be raised again'. Then they remembered his words" (vv.5-8).

It is all too easy for us to wonder how they could have forgotten, but resurrection was a totally new revelation for them to wrap their minds around. Mark records in his Gospel that when the disciples came down from the mount of transfiguration, they were discussing amongst themselves what Jesus could have meant by this talk of rising from the dead (Mark 9). They went back to the others and told them of their encounter, but were dismissed and disbelieved. Peter went to check it out for himself, but still could not comprehend what had occurred.

On the same day, two other followers of Jesus are leaving Jerusalem and heading to a town called Emmaus. They, too, are confused and despondent over what has taken place over the Passover weekend. While they are discussing this between themselves, Jesus suddenly joins them and enquires about their conversation. Throughout the Gospels, we observe Jesus expertly using questions to bring people into a greater understanding of the truth about Himself. They respond by revealing they "had hoped that he was the one who was going to redeem Israel" (v.21). They had placed their hope in a form of external redemption, whereas the redemptive work of God starts in the heart with new birth and is followed by the constant renewal of the mind through the truth of Scripture. Our transformed lives can subsequently be used by God to bring about transformation in the world.

Jesus gives them a gentle but direct rebuke when He calls them "foolish" and "slow of heart" (v.25), essentially meaning that they are not fully comprehending all that has been said in the Scriptures, and are dull of mind. While we can judge the early disciples for their inability to comprehend Jesus' words, we too run the risk of becoming so familiar with the story of Christ, the cross, and His resurrection that we fail to fully understand the impact this history-defining event should have upon us. As someone put it, we can run the risk of becoming 'gospel hardened saints.' Francis and Edith Schaeffer, in their work on the Gospel of Luke, talk about how we need to 'polish the prophecies'. We need to keep 'polishing' the Word of God so it shines brightly in our hearts and minds.

One of the most profound truths that emerge from this passage is that Jesus grounded His disciples' faith not only in the resurrection itself but also in the Word of God. At no point in His ministry did Jesus ever say, "I am here, you don't need the Scriptures any more." Exactly the opposite was true. Twice in Luke 24, we see Jesus taking His followers through all the Old Testament had to say about Him. The Word of God was to be their foundation of truth and reality, as it was to Him.

As His followers today, let's keep polishing the prophecies, so that like the disciples on the road to Emmaus, our eyes would be opened and our hearts would burn with the truth of Jesus' Word.

What verses and promises from God do you need to polish in this season? Write them out and ask God to open the eyes of your heart to truly understand and stand on His Word.

DAY FORTY

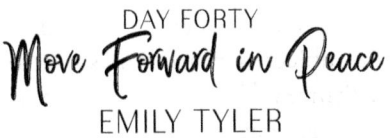

EMILY TYLER

Luke 24:36-53

My first time coxing was a baptism by fire. I found myself in a boat with eight big, burly men amidst a sea of tourist boats, ferries, water taxis, cruise liners, and even giant cargo ships. Historically known as the River Thamesis, this was my River Nemesis! The wind was picking up, the coach was barking orders through a megaphone, and the whole situation was rather turbulent. With all nine lives in the boat counting on me, I felt completely overwhelmed. I was confused, insecure, and scared. I didn't know what I was doing, and I did not 'have it together'.

I don't know if you've ever felt like that, but here the disciples were in much the same predicament. Overwhelmed and confused by the death of their Saviour and scared of the Jewish leaders (John 20:19), they are just grappling with the news that Jesus has been seen when, lo and behold, He's suddenly in the room.

Understandably they are "startled and frightened" (v.37) with doubting and troubled minds (v.38). This is the epitome of an overwhelming situation. 'Troubled' in English doesn't quite capture the original meaning of *tarasso*, literally 'shaken back and forth'. It's inward commotion, agitation, confusion, fear, trepidation, and even excitement—all of which leave the disciples unsettled and disorientated.

In verse 38, Jesus questions the doubt that arises in the disciples' hearts. However, the Greek *kardia* refers to more than simply the organ that pumps blood around your body. *Kardia* encompasses your entire being: heart (desire), mind, character, inner self, will, intention— it's *all of you*.

When we feel disorientated by our circumstances, confusion at the core of our being can trigger powerful waves of emotion that overwhelm us, making it difficult to cope. But Jesus knows this and offers what we all need in a turbulent and bewildering world: peace. A tangible, powerful, objective peace. And so, into the midst of chaos and confusion, *The* Prince of Peace arrives. From the verb *eirene*, this peace is about bringing that which is separated together. This is 'having it together' personified. Real, alive, physically present, Jesus. He is the One, the Peace, that takes you from doubt and trouble to a state of "joy and amazement"—the kind that feels too good to be true (v.41).

I survived the River Nemesis that day because of the Stroke sitting in front of me. He opened up the world of rowing to me, feeding me lines and explaining what I needed to do. And while I still felt out of my depth, as my understanding grew so did my peace.

Having something opened up to you is a reassuring feeling, and throughout chapter 24 we see many things opened: the tomb (v.12), a home (v.29), eyes (v.31), Scriptures (v.32), lips (v.35), minds (v.45), and finally, heaven itself (v.51). Embracing openness permits transparency, accessibility, freedom, and understanding. Being open allows growth and vitality—open hands, open hearts, open minds.

Jesus knew that for the disciples' emotions to return to an even keel, they would need their minds to settle also. So He met their needs not only through His Peace-bringing presence, but also by opening their minds "so they could understand" (v.45). Just as I came to enjoy the chaos of the river by understanding its whys and hows, so too did the disciples come to celebrate what once caused unrest as Jesus lovingly fed them line by line through the Scriptures, bringing clarity, calm, and confidence.

As we conclude our journey through Luke, let's remember that we have also been given access to an open Heaven of peace and joy through the promised gift of the Father (v.49; Romans 14:17). Through the power of the Spirit, we no longer need to be tossed around by the waves of an unsettled mind (James 1:6), because we have been given the "mind of Christ" (1 Corinthians 2:16)—a mind not attained through our own intellect, striving, or capacity, but gifted to us by the same power that raised Jesus from the grave. With this gift, we can move forward in peace, with settled minds, equipped and enabled to worship with "great joy" (v.52).

As you conclude this study in Luke, what truths has God revealed to you that will enable you to move forward in greater peace and joy? Thank God for the understanding He has given you and celebrate the wealth in His Word as you commit to keep your heart and mind fixed on the Prince of Peace.

Contributing Writers

We are so grateful for our writing team and the heart and wisdom that they have brought to this project. Connect with them on Instagram to read more of their work.

Vickey Bentley	@purposeful_joy
Becky Birmingham	@itsyagirlbex
Heather Carlisle	@glimpses.of.the.sanctuary
Adéle Deysel	@adeledeysel
Kay Gleaves	@becomingkaygleaves
Shelley Johnson	@shelleylinnjohnson
Mazhar Kefali	@mazharkefali
Jenna Marie Masters	@marked_by_love
Tabitha Meglich	@ajoyfulsparrow
Paula Morrison	@paula_morrison2804
Amber Palmer	@myjarsofclay
Tiffany Seldon	@tiffseldon
Victoria Stewart Malone	@beautifulfabulousfriends
Dan Tyler	@danieltylercojc
Emily Tyler	@helloemtyler
Aimée Walker	@aimeerwalker

About the Devoted Collective

Our vision is simple: to wholeheartedly pursue the 'more' of God together.

This looks like serving God with wholehearted devotion, fulfilling the command Christ gave us to love the Lord with all our heart, soul, and mind (Matthew 22:37).

We want to love God with all that we are right where we are. In order to do that, The Devoted Collective is anchored in three core disciplines modelled for us in Acts 2:42: devotion to the Word, to community, and to prayer. It is our heart's desire that, through committing to these practices with us, you will experience the richness of all God intends for your life as you come to know Him more intimately.

The more we know God, the more we can't help but love Him; and the more we love Him, the more we'll desire to partner with Him to establish it on earth as it is in Heaven. And that's what wholehearted devotion is all about. It's about living into the MORE of God.

Connect with us:

Website: www.thedevotedcollective.org
Socials: @thedevotedcollective

Join Us in the Devoted Community

We want to invite you to be part of The Devoted Community.

A curated online space hosted by Elim accredited Pastor Aimée Walker and Go + Tell Gals Certified Coach and Pastor, Em Tyler, The Devoted Community is an intentional discipleship hub, that will equip, empower, and release you into all that God has for you and help you build a resilient relationship with your God. It's where you'll find a company of women to cheer you on and a toolkit of resources to help you grow and go deeper with God.

WITHIN OUR COMMUNITY YOU WILL FIND:

Bible reading plans
Interviews & Teaching videos
Prayer threads and small groups
Dedicated mentors and monthly lives with Aimée and Emily
Access to our digital courses
Downloadable study guides & journals
Believers seeking the heart of God—just like you

WHO IS IT FOR?

If you are hungry and thirsty for more of Jesus...
If you desire to go deeper in your faith...
If you want to take hold of all the promises of God...
If you yearn for your faith to make a difference every day...
If you long to enjoy Him all the days of your life...
If you are looking for others who feel the same...

...then The Devoted Community is for you.

Let's pursue the MORE of God together:

www.thedevotedcollective.org/community

www.ingramcontent.com/pod-product-compliance
Lightning Source LLC
Chambersburg PA
CBHW051703160426
43209CB00004B/997